# SOLDIERS FIRST

# SOLDIERS FIRST

*Duty, Honor, Country, and*
*Football at West Point*

## JOE DRAPE

TIMES BOOKS

Henry Holt and Company  New York

Times Books
Henry Holt and Company, LLC
*Publishers since 1866*
175 Fifth Avenue
New York, New York 10010

Henry Holt® is a registered trademark of
Henry Holt and Company, LLC.

Library of Congress Cataloging-in-Publication Data

Drape, Joe.
    Soldiers first : duty, honor, country, and football at West Point / Joe Drape.
        p. cm.
    Includes index.
    ISBN 978-0-8050-9490-9 (hardback)
    1. United States Military Academy—Football—History.   2. United States
Corps of Cadets—History.   I. Title.
    GV958.U5D74 2012
    796.332'630974731—dc23

                                                            2012013054

Henry Holt books are available for special promotions and
premiums. For details contact: Director, Special Markets.

First Edition 2012

*Designed by Kelly S. Too*

Printed in the United States of America
1 3 5 7 9 10 8 6 4 2

*For Mary and Jack*
*Every day with you is better than the last*

# ·CONTENTS·

# SOLDIERS FIRST

# PROLOGUE

———•————————•———

> "Let's go see the good guys, Dad."
>
> —Jack Drape, November 20, 2010

It was my five-year-old son, Jack, who took me to the banks of the Hudson River and the United States Military Academy at West Point, New York. Our journey started with a pizza and a football game one November evening in 2010, when his mother was out and we were having a bachelor night at home in Manhattan. Lucky for us, Notre Dame was facing Army on national television in the brand-new Yankee Stadium about five miles north of us in the Bronx. I am a Fighting Irish fan by virtue of growing up Catholic in the Midwest, having an uncle who taught at Notre Dame for more than thirty-five years and a brother who graduated from the university. We were frequent visitors to South Bend, Indiana, and our trips usually revolved around a football game.

In fact, Jack had already made the pilgrimage to Notre Dame Stadium the previous season and nearly witnessed an upset of the University of Southern California. He was already conversant about Touchdown Jesus, the Grotto, and most things Golden Dome.

None of that mattered, however, as soon as he saw the Corps of Cadets marching into Yankee Stadium in a long gray line. They marched as one, as simply and eloquently as the motto embedded in West Point's coat of arms: Duty, Honor, Country. Jack was so captivated that he climbed on top of the couch and watched the rest of the broadcast's pregame in total thrall. He laughed in utter delight when members of the U.S. Army Black Daggers parachute team sailed into the stadium with the Army flag, the Notre Dame flag, and finally the game ball for what was going to be the first matchup between the two teams in Yankee Stadium since 1969. He listened to Pete Dawkins, who won the Heisman Trophy in 1958 as a member of Army's last undefeated team, explain how Army football was different, how it defined who we are as a nation.

"Honor—its place is at the very core of the United States Military Academy and it can be felt every time the Army football team takes the field," said Dawkins. "Honor is about commitment. Commitment to a cause. Commitment to one another. It's about sacrifice and dedication in a level that goes far beyond wins and losses on the football field.

"We pursue the game because we love it. We play the game because it prepares us, and we cherish the game because it defines who we are. Tonight, Army takes the field at Yankee Stadium . . . tonight, honor triumphs once more."

By the time the Black Knights emerged from the locker room in their white jerseys and gold helmets and pants, Jack was vibrating out of his skin. He howled as each of the Black Knights pounded the placard held reverently by an Army colonel, bearing the words of one of the greatest American generals of all time, George C. Marshall: "I want an officer for a secret and dangerous mission," Marshall said during World War II. "I want a West Point football player."

From then on, Notre Dame never had a chance. Jack had a new favorite team.

"Let's go see the good guys, Dad," he said to me.

I got it. He wanted to see in flesh and blood his "Army guys," the little green plastic soldiers for whom he spent hours building bases and air fields and leading them through the treacherous terrain of his bedroom floor. I had grown up with them, most of us had, projecting all manner of virtues and bravery onto them as they battled evil enemies. Jack loved his "Army guys." He still does. Now, before him on the television screen, he saw real good guys, who marched with purpose and jumped out of planes with abandon and played football, too. Jack had to see them up close. Meet them. He had to know they were as good and as brave as the troops he commanded in his imagination. Sometimes it takes the eyes of a child to open our own, and the joy the Black Knights were bringing to my son stirred something in my soul.

I had impressions of the military rather than any firsthand experience. I was a boy during Vietnam and remember my mom cutting vegetables in the kitchen, watching Walter Cronkite on her eight-inch Sony television talk about body counts and looking terribly sad. My cousin Rick was in ROTC in college, became a pilot in the Air Force, and retired as a lieutenant colonel after twenty-two years. He is a good guy with a commanding presence. And he is proud of his service. As a young reporter during the first Gulf War, I had been to Fort Bragg and Camp Lejeune in North Carolina for various stories, and the soldiers and the officers I met were precise and straightforward.

As a parent in our conflict-ridden post–September 11 world, I have regarded soldiers with gratitude, admiration, and respect. I also understand that they are someone's sons or daughters and need our prayers and support.

What I knew too much about, however, was college sports, especially big-time college football, and what a strange, unhealthy, and phenomenally profitable organism it had become. I was a student at Southern Methodist University in the early 1980s when the governor of Texas, Bill Clements, and members of the university's board of directors built the best football team money could buy with a slush fund that lavished tens of thousands of dollars on players even as the program was already serving a two-year NCAA (National Collegiate Athletic Association) probation. It paid off. From 1980 to 1986, SMU won sixty-one games, captured two conference championships outright, and tied for another. But then the hammer came down—hard. On February 25, 1987, my alma mater became the first and only college football program to be given the so-called death penalty and was shut down for a year by the NCAA, and then for a second year by the university itself.

It took the SMU football program more than two decades to recover from that blow. The Mustangs did not return to a bowl game until 2009. But the death penalty hardly acted as a deterrent for the rest of the big college football programs. The University of Alabama, Ohio State, Auburn University, the University of North Carolina, and the University of Miami are among a long who's who list of institutions of higher education that had lost control of their football programs and were paying for it with sordid headlines about payments to players or other rules violations. No amount of public embarrassment, however, has seemed to affect the bottom lines of college football teams.

By the fall of 2010, the Big Ten Conference was nearly halfway through a ten-year, $1 billion broadcast contract with ABC/ESPN, and analysts projected that it would be worth twice that when it was up for renewal in 2016. The Big Ten had also built its own network that was six years into a twenty-five-year $2.8 billion agreement with Fox Broadcasting that not only was already generating more than $235 million annually in revenues but was changing the face of the college sports landscape. Conferences like the former Pac-10 and the Big East and individual universities like Texas now wanted their own networks and were willing to abandon longtime allegiances to get them. By 2011 Nebraska would throw in with the Big Ten, and Colorado and Utah left the Big 12 and the Mountain West for the Pac-10. It was simply confusing to be a college football fan. The Big Ten was about to have twelve teams, the Big 12 only ten, and the Pacific-10 was now twelve teams and really wished it had sixteen.

This was happening even though all but 14 of the 120 athletic programs in the Football Bowl Subdivision—the highest level of college sports—had lost money in the previous academic year. The year prior to that, 25 programs had turned a profit, according to the NCAA. It didn't matter that the country was suffering through a recession. Overall spending among these schools was up 11 percent, and the universities themselves increased their contribution to athletics by 28 percent.

Just four months earlier, in the summer of 2010, I had gone to Gainesville, where the University of Florida had laid off 139 faculty and staff members over the previous two and a half years in response to a cut in state funding of more than $150 million. But the first thing I saw was three dozen Gator football players, presumably on campus for summer school but mostly to practice unofficially, zipping around campus on nearly identical motor scooters. I don't know how the players got scooters—they could have rented or borrowed them or even owned them outright. It was clear, however, that the football players were the princes of the campus—hell, the whole state—and if they needed some transportation to ease their summer camp experience in the north Florida heat they got it. Why not? Jeremy Foley, Florida's athletic director, oversaw a budget of almost $95 million. He made $1.2 million a year, and his football coach, Urban Meyer, took home $4.5 million. Both men had three private planes at their disposal. Foley had just renovated a football center that was not only state-of-the-art in its facility and amenities but also certified as an eco-friendly "green building." It was just one of nearly a dozen tricked-out stadiums and athletic training centers that were among the most prized on campus.

Florida is hardly alone in its excessive and expensive devotion to its college football team. Over the past fifteen years as a sportswriter, most of it covering colleges, I have written about so-called student-athletes beating up their girlfriends, tutors writing athletes' papers, and professors giving As for the good old U's football players in every corner of the country. How corrupt is college sports? All you need to know is that there are law firms that bill hundreds of millions of dollars annually to universities to investigate the abuses of their athletic programs, making the charges go away when possible or negotiating a lesser sentence from the NCAA.

No one should be surprised that many of these law firms were founded by and stocked with former NCAA employees.

Even as Jack and I were settling in for the Army–Notre Dame game, college football was awash in more scandal. The University of Southern California had been banned from the postseason for two years and had to vacate thirteen victories, including the Orange Bowl victory that gave them the 2004 national title, after investigators determined that players had received illegal benefits and that USC had lost all "institutional control." The Trojans' former star running back Reggie Bush had just returned the Heisman Trophy he earned as the nation's outstanding player in 2005 after NCAA investigators found that he may have taken more than $300,000 in cash and benefits from an agent.

The fate of Cam Newton, the Auburn quarterback and Heisman Trophy favorite, was also up in the air as the NCAA investigated whether Newton's father, Cecil, had offered his son's talents to Mississippi State in exchange for $180,000 in cash. In Columbus, Ohio, a federal investigation was under way into an alleged drug trafficker and money launderer who got memorabilia from five Ohio State players in exchange for cash and tattoos. The beloved coach Jim Tressell knew about the investigation and his players' involvement, but he did not pass the information on to school officials, a transgression that led him to resign under pressure.

And we didn't know it yet, but the worst was still to come. A year later, in the fall of 2011, a grand jury in State College, Pennsylvania, would hear evidence of how a former Penn State assistant football coach, Jerry Sandusky, had allegedly molested at least eight boys. When forty counts were subsequently filed against Sandusky, and testimony emerged that Penn State officials had known about the allegations but had not contacted law enforcement, university president Graham Spanier, athletic director Tim Curley, and the Nittany Lions' iconic football coach Joe Paterno were fired and their reputations left in ruins.

Where did honor reside anymore in college football? From atop the back of our couch, mouth agape, Jack was pointing me to the banks of the Hudson River and the historic military academy that rightly has earned the reputation as a national treasure. I knew little about West Point as an institution of higher learning beyond the fact it was hard to get into, rigorous once you were there, and was free only if you looked past the fact that its students were required to serve five years in the Army after graduation.

I knew the basics of Army football's history, and now NBC's pregame show was reminding me of the highlights: They were undefeated national champions in 1944 and 1945 under the legendary head coach Red Blaik. Three Army football players had won the Heisman Trophy—Doc Blanchard ('45), Glenn Davis ('46), and Dawkins. And, along with Notre Dame, Army was considered a football powerhouse for the first half of the twentieth century. The Fighting Irish and Black Knights met twenty-one times between 1925 and 1946, and tonight was the fiftieth time they were facing each other.

The current edition of Black Knights brought a 6–4 record into their contest with the Fighting Irish and would be good enough for the team to be eligible for a bowl game for the first time in fifteen years. When the opening kickoff came and Jack declared he was for Army, my mind was made up.

I was ready to go see some good guys myself.

# PART ONE

# PLEBE YEAR

# 1

"One, two, three, stay together; three, two, one, sing second!"
—The Army Black Knights, February 16, 2011

It was the first day of spring football practice, though the snow piled outside Foley Athletic Center and the chunks of ice tumbling in the Hudson River below the United States Military Academy suggested otherwise. It is on cold, wintry days like these that West Point looks more like the oldest continually utilized United States Army post than the nation's premier leader-development institute. It's easy to imagine these highlands teeming with Revolutionary War soldiers, picks and shovels in hand, building a garrison here in 1778 under Tadeusz Kosciuszko. George Washington himself assigned Kosciuszko to keep the Hudson from the Redcoats, and the Polish general did so with a feat of engineering that turned narrow mountain trails and ridgetop strongholds, along with a one-hundred-ton iron chain stretched across the river, into an impenetrable fort.

He did such a good job that Benedict Arnold pursued and landed command of West Point in 1780 so he could surrender it to the British. The plot failed, of course, as Arnold became America's most famous traitor, but ever since this place has been regarded with a sense of mystery and magic.

West Point is rooted in our founding fathers—Alexander Hamilton, John Adams, and George Washington pushed to create a United States Military Academy, and it was President Thomas Jefferson who signed the legislation establishing it in 1802. Its immediate contributions were the engineers sent out into our wildernesses to build roads and railways, bridges and harbors, to lay the scaffolding of a growing nation. While the goal always was to create a professional officer class—leaders, strategists, and warriors—West Point became good at it out of necessity.

Its graduates are found throughout our history books, synonymous with some of America's greatest achievements. Ulysses S. Grant and Robert E. Lee fought brilliantly in the Mexican War before finding themselves on opposite sides in the Civil War. Dwight D. Eisenhower was the supreme allied commander in Europe during World War II before becoming our thirty-fourth president. Alexander M. Haig Jr. was secretary of state under President Ronald Reagan. Brent Scowcroft was the national security adviser under Presidents Gerald Ford and George H. W. Bush. Buzz Aldrin was the lunar module pilot of Apollo 11, the first manned lunar landing in history. Norman Schwarzkopf Jr. was the commander of coalition forces in the first Gulf War. These members of the "Long Gray Line"—and many, many more—not only have decided how we have fought our wars but have shaped how we, as well as the rest of the world, see ourselves as a nation.

Coach Rich Ellerson knew this history chapter and verse. Better, he felt it deeply. He spoke as enthusiastically as my son,

Jack, about the company he was keeping here on the banks of the Hudson, the good guys who were his players. What they lacked in size and skill they made up for with heart. Notre Dame beat Army that night in Yankee Stadium, 21–3, and it was clear the Black Knights were no match physically or athletically for the much bigger and faster Fighting Irish. Army perhaps had five or six players that might play special teams or rise to third or second string at Notre Dame or at any of the other traditional college powers. Still, for all sixty minutes, Army played hard and determined and in utter denial that they were outclassed athletically. Their performance just made me more curious. I wanted to know where, if at all, did football fit in at West Point and whether the young men on the Black Knights were soldiers or football players first.

Ellerson is a football coach, an innovative one who had climbed the coaching rungs over the past thirty-two years, turning gigs at backwaters like Arizona Western College into better ones at the University of Idaho and the University of Hawaii. He detoured into the Canadian Football League, soaking up everything about teaching young men the nuances of the game, before landing at the University of Arizona and the big leagues of college football for most of the 1990s.

At fifty-seven years old Ellerson was not a young man, and when he was named Army's thirty-sixth head football coach he was hardly an obvious choice. He brought a solid record of 60–41 as a head coach, but his victories mostly had been racked up far from the limelight at California Polytechnic State University in San Luis Obispo, a Division 1-AA school better known for turning out topflight engineers and architects than National Football League prospects.

As we sat in Coach Ellerson's office, however, it was clear

he was not only the best choice but perhaps the only one to try to revive a once-proud program that frankly had become embarrassing to watch. Army had not posted a winning record since 1996 and had been a dismal 35–115 before Ellerson arrived in 2009. Worse, the Black Knights managed to lose to Navy in ten of the previous twelve years, allowing the Midshipmen to gain an unforgivable 55–49–7 edge in the nation's most storied college football rivalry. The four coaches who preceded Ellerson were hardly slouches. Stan Brock had played fifteen years in the NFL. Bobby Ross had won a share of the 1990 national championship when he was head coach at Georgia Tech and, in the 1994 season, he had taken the San Diego Chargers to Super Bowl XXIX. Todd Berry had coached Illinois State to the Division 1-AA semifinals in 1999 and was currently the head coach of the University of Louisiana at Monroe. Bob Sutton went 10–2 and took Army to a bowl game in 1996, but after winning just nine more games over the next three seasons he was fired and now coached defense for the New York Jets.

What Ellerson had and they didn't, however, was a genuine connection to West Point. He nodded to the wall of his office where a portrait of his father as a cadet hung: Colonel Geoffrey Ellerson graduated from West Point in 1935. Opposite it was a photograph of the 1962 Army team, captained by his brother Major General (Ret.) John Ellerson ('63). There was a framed photo on his desk of another brother, Colonel (Ret.) Geoffrey Ellerson Jr. ('63). His nephew Colonel Geoffrey Ellerson III had served in Iraq and was soon to be deployed to Afghanistan. Ellerson had grown up on bases around the world and had listened to Army games on shortwave radios. He wore his hair as high and tight as any cadet and already had traveled to American bases in Iraq and Afghanistan in his off-seasons to meet former West Point officers and their troops.

Ellerson understood West Point. He had grown up with duty, honor, and country. He understood, too, how much football meant to the whole of the Army. "More than any other place in America, this is an important job," Ellerson told me. "This is the United States Military Academy. We're playing football. We need to be good at this. We need to be. Everybody wants to win. We *need* to."

Ellerson had chased this job and was among the first candidates to call and put his name into contention. His Cal Poly teams ran the triple-option offense, a staple of service academy football programs because it rewards poise and precision, which cadets possess in greater supply than they do speed, size, and strength. He also was the architect of a novel defense, the double-eagle flex, which depended on quick thinking and fluid movement to create the organized chaos that often tamed bigger, faster, and far more talented teams. It had powered the University of Arizona into the top ranks of college football, and in the early 1990s Ellerson had come east to West Point to help Coach Sutton install a version of what was known then as the Desert Swarm defense.

His acumen with the right kind of X's and O's got his foot in the door, but he was intent on kicking it down. Ellerson, a six-foot-three former linebacker, doesn't merely fill up a room, he commands it. He speaks in full paragraphs and vibrates with the energy and certitude of a preacher. In December 2008, in a hotel conference room in Washington, D.C., he bowled over the athletic director, Kevin Anderson, and a selection committee of former graduates and players. He promised them that his cadets would balance an Ivy League–caliber education with the rigors of military life as they absorbed the art and science of leadership. He assured them that the Black Knights would compete on the football field in a way that would make every one of them, and every West Point grad in the Pentagon or a dusty desert barracks or corporate boardroom, proud. He told them that Army football could be good again.

Ellerson's passion—no, insistence—that he was going to embrace the academy's mission of building character and contribute to his players' education as officers had rarely been heard from the recent denizens of the Kimsey Athletic Center, the state-of-the-art home of the football program. No, previous regimes wanted West Point's admission requirements altered so that their three-hundred-pound linemen could be admitted even if they were unable to complete the fitness test mandatory for all cadets. They wanted football players to be granted more time for practice and to carry lighter academic loads. They also wanted the players to be excused from the military training obligations.

"We are not going to win in spite of West Point," Ellerson told the selection committee. "We are going to win because of West Point. We are going to march with our units and be first in line for formation in the mornings. We are going to study hard, learn how to jump out of planes. We are going to make sure we're pulling in the same direction that everyone else is on post. We are going to validate our Academy experience to the point where I can say that part of our success on Saturday afternoons is directly attributable to their Cadet Basic Training, their Cadet Field Training, or their Cadet Leader Training."

So far Ellerson had delivered. He assembled a staff on the fly, hiring a half dozen coaches he had worked with on the West Coast and at Cal Poly, and keeping another dozen already on the Army staff. They threw together a recruiting class and in spring practice began to install a new offense, a new defense, and a new attitude. In 2009, Army went 5–7—the most victories in a season for the Black Knights since 1996. In 2010, Army finished 7–6 and beat SMU in the Armed Forces Bowl, the Academy's first postseason victory since 1985.

Beyond running an offense and a defense built on speed and flexibility, Ellerson was tapping into the values and virtues of West Point off the field. He had coached smart kids at Cal Poly and understood how time was the most precious commodity of the highly motivated. Still, his cadets were buried in schoolwork, had bags under their eyes, but remained focused and were eager to absorb what he offered. Ellerson did what he could to help. He practiced just three days a week and rarely held all-out full-contact drills.

"These guys are so invested emotionally in this place," he said. "It's so demanding. It's so uncertain. It's so competitive. I don't think there is that emotional investment for kids playing at Tennessee or Texas or the places with the big Hollywood models. They are there mainly for Saturdays."

Ellerson had moved spring practice up to the dead of winter in the hope that his team could maintain conditioning before the beer drinking of spring break gave way to the grueling military exercises of the summer. He confessed that he was far from "cracking the code" of West Point, which meant figuring out how to keep his players well fed, rested, and injury free. Ellerson loved being Army's football coach. He recognized how daunting were the challenges, but he was inspired by his players.

"There's some physics going on out there. How you can counter it is with culture and character," he said. "These are guys that are willing to sacrifice for one another. They want to do something special with their life. They don't want their life to be easy or pampered. It's not in our DNA."

Ellerson was troubled, too. He wanted his current players and incoming recruits to understand exactly why they were coming to the United States Military Academy: to become Army officers. He had been surprised how many of the players he had inherited said that they had come here to play big-time college football.

"The destination is the first thing we bring up," he said. "Where it goes from here probably is to many, many great things. This silly game we all love—football—is just one thing on the way to the destination."

Ellerson was a parent, after all. He and his wife, Dawn, had raised four children and their youngest, Andrew, was a senior in high school and would be attending the United States Military Academy Prep School in the fall to prepare with other high schoolers, as well as with promising Army enlisted personnel, for their appointments to West Point. Andrew was a wide receiver and a long snapper, but Ellerson made damn sure Andrew knew that the goal and the endgame of attending West Point was to become a second lieutenant in the world's greatest Army.

Ellerson had been around football and kids long enough to know that what they promise with their lips may not be what's beating in their hearts. He only needed to look back to his own collegiate career. He was not only an Army brat but an Army football brat who had idolized his older brothers and scheduled his autumn Saturdays around the Black Knights' kickoffs. But when West Point did not recruit him to play football as it did his older brother John, Ellerson accepted an appointment at Navy. He loved football and he thought he was better at it than he was. He lasted only a year at Navy before transferring to the University of Hawaii, where he played linebacker and found a starting position at center. Ellerson had ended up with a peripatetic career, just not a military one. What happened? Ellerson's sheepish answer hinted at regret but fell squarely on being young and dumb. "I was nineteen—I had no excuse, sir," he said, echoing the answer a cadet gives when found doing something unacceptable.

Now, forty years later, Ellerson was getting a do-over at West Point. Army football may not have had a vision for him when he was a high school senior, but Ellerson had a powerful one that he intended to implement at West Point in the coming days, months, and years. He wasn't so much turning back the clock as trying to build a football program for the future, one that resonated beyond the Hudson, with any young football player or coach or sports fan who valued honorable competition.

"This is a great job," he said. "It's a hard job, and what we are doing here is still a work in progress, but it's important work."

The short-term, as well as long-term, challenges for Army football were immense. During spring practice, Ellerson and his staff were trying to cope with the fact that four of the five starting offensive linemen were soon to graduate. The defense was in even worse shape—six standout starters had to be replaced, including Stephen Anderson, the Black Knights' leading tackler and emotional leader, as well as Josh McNary, Army's all-time leader in tackles for loss and quarterback sacks. Seasoned senior replacements were in short supply as the Black Knights' "Firstie" class, as seniors are known, was a compact one—seventeen of them, many battling injuries. The "Cow," or junior, class Ellerson had inherited was thin on Division I–caliber talent.

He and his staff really had only two classes of recruits to

call their own and had upgraded Army's athleticism remark-
ably. Having to rely on freshmen and sophomores, however,
usually means a long learning curve and, more than likely, a
losing season for any Division I college football team. At Army,
this situation was beyond perilous. The freshmen were sleep-
deprived, harassed, and overwhelmed just trying to survive
their "Plebe" year. For the sophomores, known as "Yearlings,"
or "Yuks," the hardships were more existential. "Now that I
survived the Plebe's year of hell," they asked themselves, "do I
want to continue down the Army way?" Cadets had the choice
not to continue at the Academy after sophomore year and
leave honorably with their credits. If they decided to withdraw
after that, however, they would owe Uncle Sam two years in
the Army, to make good for two years of free education.

Then there was the matter of Army's schedule for the upcoming 2011 season. It was brutal. The Black Knights opened with
three teams coming out of bowl games: Northern Illinois had
crushed Fresno State in the Humanitarian Bowl; San Diego
State had walloped Navy in the Poinsettia Bowl; and Northwestern University had narrowly lost a shoot-out with Texas
Tech in the TicketCity Bowl.

For now, however, there were more pressing matters that
needed Ellerson's attention. It was a Thayer Week, a stretch of
testing and projects named for Colonel Sylvanus Thayer, who
became the superintendent in 1817 and created the curricu-
lum still in use. The coach had been notified that a few of his
players were struggling with their studies. He not only dismissed them from spring practice but sent their instructors
e-mails telling them he had done so in order to "send a message to all concerned that we are dead serious about winning in
every domain." The chasm between the football program and
the rest of the Academy was not of Ellerson's making, but he

was committed to bridging it and demonstrating that the football program was in lockstep with the culture of West Point.

"Stacking Ws" is what he exhorted his players to do in all their activities as cadets—in the barracks, on the parade field, and during the summer missions. "Winning is a habit, and you got to do it all day," he said. "You just can't flick a switch on on Saturdays."

His guys were starting to get it. He waved some e-mails in the air that he had recently received from an officer in the chemistry department, saying that sixty-seven of his football players were more than holding their own; they had posted an 84 percent average. Another professor wanted to be sure that Ellerson knew that four of his freshmen football players had been selected as part of the Plebe-Parent weekend chain of command.

"It is obvious that the Plebes on your team have internalized the team's core virtues and are truly making an effort to win in every aspect of cadet life," wrote a major who taught military movement to nine freshmen football players in his class. "Each of these cadets demonstrated tremendous teamwork with the rest of the class and consistently set an outstanding example with their attitude."

Ellerson was gratified, but there was much more to do. He vaulted from his chair and led me to a door with "War Room" stenciled on it. He then ushered me into a conference room with floor-to-ceiling whiteboards. The names of his players—130 of them—popped from the whiteboards in a Technicolor rainbow. It wasn't a depth chart of who was expected to play where next fall. It was a log of his players' military assignments for the summer. The Firsties were in yellow, the Cows in blue, the Yearlings in red, and the Plebes in green. I could see that quarterback Trent Steelman would spend part of this summer at nearby Camp Buckner leading a squad of ten cadets through combat exercises, while his backup, Max Jenkins, would be in Germany with the Army Corps of Engineers, and defensive lineman Jarrett Mackey was among a group of players in infantry training at Fort Benning, Georgia. The Plebes? Well, they would be confined to Beast Barracks, or Cadet Basic Training, where they would be drilled on everything from fitness and weaponry to military manners and knowledge. It was otherwise known as "Hell on the Hudson." Ellerson's whiteboard kept track of not only the players' whereabouts on different bases and missions but also those of the strength coaches, whom Ellerson was deploying to keep his guys in some semblance of football shape.

Ellerson raised a finger and tapped names on each of the walls. "This is the kind of company I keep," he said, "Young men who spend 365 days a year learning to be leaders. Who, when they leave here, have committed five years of their life to go into dangerous places and defend our country with their lives."

Twenty minutes later, Ellerson gathered his team at the 50-yard line of the practice field, and the steam from the breaths of 130 would-be officers wafted in the air like it came from a blazing bonfire. The coach congratulated them on the accomplishments of the past year but reminded them what was left before them to overcome. He waded into the knot of cadets, holding one hand in the air.

"For two years now, we've put our hands together before and after every practice and game and said, 'Bring it back,'" he said, his voice cracking with emotion. "You guys have done that, and I'm proud you, and the Corps and the men and women of the Army are proud. Now it's time to take this thing up another level."

His players pressed closer and reached their hands toward

his, piling into one another, elbows on shoulders, fingers on wrists. "On three, we're going to say, 'Sing second,' " he said.

The Black Knights roared. They understood exactly the mission their coach had set out before them. Each December, at the conclusion of the Army-Navy game, the two teams gather before their respective corps and alumni to sing their alma maters. The losers go first; the victors sing second. Army hadn't had that privilege for nine years.

"One, two, three, stay together; three, two, one, sing second!" they roared. It echoed like cannon fire on the banks of the Hudson.

# 2

> "When you're in charge, be in charge. Make a decision. Don't worry if it's the right or wrong one; make the decision."
>
> —Steve Erzinger, June 19, 2011

Steve Erzinger wanted out of the United States Military Academy after his Plebe year. He had marched until blisters formed on his feet, and he had hated every minute of it. He didn't like the upperclass cadets in his face, demanding "knowledge," the necessary and often arcane oaths, rules, and history that Plebes must recite about all things military. He had been prepared for the harassment that is a Plebe's constant companion. When he was weighing the pros and cons of attending West Point, a family friend had introduced him to Tom White, a member of West Point's class of 1967. He was a retired general with a great deal of wisdom to offer but none that Steve appreciated more than his prescription for surviving Plebe year.

"Don't be a hero and don't be a goat," White told him. "When someone asks you to do something, get it done quickly. You don't want them to know your name—because then they'll either always be calling on you to do something or blaming you for something."

There were no shortcuts or sage strategies for getting the best of West Point's academic demands short of studying your tail off. Steve had been a sharp but uninspired student at Lamar High School in Houston, Texas. He was savvy enough to bear down in spurts, but he had skipped classes when he could and, most days, left his books in his locker after school. He was a read-and-remember-and-cram kind of student come test times.

Still, Steve had a polished enough résumé to get into West Point. He suspected, however, that the fact that he had been an All-State linebacker in football-crazed Texas had not hurt his cause.

When Stan Brock was fired as Army's coach at the end of Erzinger's freshman season, Steve thought he was ready to take the "C's for degrees" that he had managed to obtain as a Plebe and transfer to a school back in his native Texas. His twin brother, Scott, was a left-handed relief pitcher for Texas Tech, and his best buddies from high school were at the University of Texas. They texted and called often to torment him about how cold the beer was, how hot the women were, and what a good time they were all having.

Now here it was June 2011, and "Erz," as his teammates called him, was a Firstie wrapping up CLDT, Cadet Leader Development Training. He was fully armed with an M4 carbine over one shoulder and an M240 Bravo machine gun at the ready. Erz's face was so dirty he didn't need to paint on any camouflage. In a rucksack on his back, he had been hoisting forty pounds, for three weeks now, traversing the woods of Camp Buckner, part of the seventeen thousand acres in the Hudson Highlands that comprise the United States Military

Academy. He had endured the near one-hundred-degree heat by day and tried his best to catch a couple of hours of sleep at night when he was bivouacked with his squad. It wasn't easy. This was the last and most intense part of his summer military training at West Point, and Erz was a dazed and battered soul.

While the linebackers at Baylor University were dividing their time between the weight room and summer school classes, and the wide receivers and running backs at Southern Methodist University were doing seven-on-seven passing drills and enjoying the nightlife along Greenville Avenue in Dallas, Erzinger and his teammates were fully engaged in learning how to lead soldiers in combat. Both Baylor and SMU wanted Erz to play for them out of high school and, in the depths of his Plebe year, he was certain he could revive their interest. He had been a standout on Army's special teams and had logged enough time as a backup linebacker to become one of only four Plebes to earn a varsity letter. Erz was listed in the program at six foot two and 221 pounds, but in the flesh he was just a hair below six feet and was perhaps 210 pounds in full pads. In fact, in the midst of his military training, Erz often dropped below 200 pounds. He was fast and aggressive, though, and he was certain that a true off-season of weight lifting at a real football school could bulk him up.

His mind was made up until he started listening to Chuck Eason, John Plumstead, and Frank Scappaticci, the Firstie linebackers who had taken Erz under their wing and taught him about playing college football. None of them had taken to West Point easily—few do—but they had persevered. Plumstead and Scappaticci had risen to become captains on the football team. In the spring semester of Erzinger's Plebe year, the trio switched their focus from football and tried to teach Steve what being a cadet really meant. Each had hated his Plebe year; they told him rare is the cadet who enjoys the year of being a doormat. They understood he was not a natural student, but they assured him that he could learn to study efficiently. What they told Erz was that he should not walk away from a first-rate education and the opportunity to soak up the military training and the experience of enduring pressure to lead soldiers well.

"You won't like everything here, but eventually you will value and appreciate it," they told him.

Erz respected them. They reminded him why he had chosen West Point. Uninterested in studies at first, Steve had made it through a year that had been challenging and stimulating in a way that he suspected drinking beer and chasing girls with his old buddies was not. It had meant a lot to Steve when Plumstead and the others told him that they did not really know it themselves when they were Plebes. He realized that he was not alone.

"What we do is important," Erz conceded almost sheepishly. "If I snapped an ACL tomorrow, I'd have a whole lot more than football to carry me through the rest of life."

So Erz rededicated himself to the books and clocked a 2.9 grade point average as a Yearling and followed that with a 3.1 as a Cow. He discovered that he did enjoy learning after all, a trait that ran in his family. His dad, Frank, had master's degrees in chemical engineering and business; his mom, Kathy, had a master's in education and was an administrator in the Houston Independent School District. His oldest sister, Alison, had earned a master's in mechanical engineering and his other sister, Stephanie, was in medical school at the University of North Texas. Erz was going to earn a degree in management from West Point and eventually wanted to pursue an MBA as his dad had done.

His football had hardly suffered, either. Erz had started twenty-five consecutive games and in 2010 was the Black Knights' second leading tackler. He also had been named Army's legacy captain by the departing Firsties, who picked one rising senior to lead the Black Knights into spring practice and beyond. The legacy captain had been instituted by Ellerson in the hope that strong ties would be forged between classes and that it would result in high standards. Of all his classmates, the departing seniors of the best Army football team in decades had selected him as the one to carry on their tradition and success. It had taken Steve aback. Erz was not a firebrand on or off the field. He wasn't physically imposing, and a square jaw and dimples framed his easy smile. When he was out of his pads, you'd mistake him for a lacrosse player or even a swimmer. He did, however, possess a quiet confidence and surety of spirit that usually was found in sherpas or fishing guides—you followed because they acted like they knew what they were doing.

Here in the woods of Camp Buckner, Erz understood that Eason, Plumstead, and Scappaticci had also been right about the military training at West Point, how it prepared him to find reserves of strength and leadership that he never knew he possessed. It suited him. It was one thing to whiteboard a scenario and walk through it, as Erz and his classmates had done scores of times in the classrooms of West Point. It was a whole other reality, however, to be sleep-deprived, disoriented, and under fire on a battlefield with the fate of a company of soldiers in your hands.

The Blackhawk helicopters thundering overhead were real, as was the Pashto and Dari chatter Erz was hearing from the Muslim American actors who had been brought to West Point

and paid to portray villagers and insurgents. They wore keffi-
yehs and bandannas on their heads and treated the Americans
with distrust and hostility. The rounds that erupted in staccato
bursts and echoed in the woods were not real, but they created
the menace and chaos that might be found on an unfamiliar
battlefield. It was as close an approximation of the perils faced
in Afghanistan or Iraq that Erz and his classmates were going
to get. Every one of their instructors had been deployed in
combat and was here to create stress for the cadets and ultimately judge their talent for leadership.

The instructors weren't there to tell them what to do, however, and that meant Steve and the other Firsties had suffered
their share of uncomfortable moments. On the first day of
CLDT, Erz was made second-in-command of his platoon of
forty soldiers and charged with establishing a base. He spent
most of his day running through the woods telling one squad
to secure the perimeter, another to set up operations, and
another to embark on reconnaissance. Back and forth Erz went
until he was sweaty, out of breath, and addled.

His instructor finally interceded.

"Why didn't you use the radios and call your squad leaders?" the officer asked.

"No excuse, sir," Erz answered.

He had overlooked the obvious—a common pitfall of
would-be officers. Another theme that the real Army colonels,
majors, captains, lieutenants, and sergeants hammered home
to the cadets was, "When you're in charge, be in charge." It is
perhaps another obvious-sounding precept, but being in command does not always come naturally to cadets.

"Make a decision" became a mantra for Erz. "Don't worry
if it's the right or wrong one; make the decision."

Now, on the final day of CLDT, Erz was the platoon leader
for the Quick Reaction Force. He had command of four squads,
or forty soldiers, and his assignment was to establish security
in a neighboring town that had fallen into insurgent hands.
For five days now, the platoon had been running missions out
of a combat outpost, or COP. His troops' nerves were frayed
and adrenaline was running low. It was 1:00 a.m. when a radio
call came in alerting him of a disturbance under way in the village. Erz and his platoon groped through the dark, walking as
if every step could be their last. He waved two squads over to
secure the perimeter and pressed on even more quietly and care-
fully with the remaining two.

Once Erz arrived in the village, time and terror moved
faster than it ever had in a football game. The insurgents had
villagers on their knees with rifles pointed at their heads. The
babble in a strange tongue was unnerving, but Erz and everyone else knew the insurgents were threatening to execute them
all. Erz ordered the translator to begin a dialogue with the
man who looked like the leader. The insurgent listened briefly,
but then he opened fire on the hostages. Erz called for backup,
but as soon as a second squad appeared more insurgents
emerged from the rooftop and popped off machine-gun fire.
There were perhaps ten of them in all. Hand grenades rolled
toward the American trucks. It was a trap. The platoon was
surrounded, and the cadets had little choice but to fight their
way out.

Erz was pressed against the wall of a Quonset hut, piecing
together radio reports amid machine-gun bursts as his soldiers
zigzagged from one fallen comrade to another, trying to drag
them to safety. Then, another call came over the radio: the
COP they had just left had been overrun and was no longer in

American control. Erz understood immediately that there was nowhere to go and that he and his platoon had to push the insurgents out and make the village their new base. There were enemy machine gunners on the roof and insurgent mortar fire was raining down on the village.

Erz and his troops caught a break when they inherited another twenty-five men who had been separated from their own platoon when the COP was taken over, and had been wandering through the woods. They helped secure half the town, enabling Erz to send out an eight-man team to search for the insurgent spotter who had been calling in the mortar fire. They found him and another insurgent on a hill overlooking the town, three hundred meters away. No wonder they had been able to land the mortars with precision. Erz's squad took them out. By 3:00 a.m. the village was back in American control.

Erz and his men had taken heavy casualties in a scenario that the instructors had designed for him and his troops to fail. There had been few good choices to make, but Erz made enough of them to save half of his platoon and secure a new American base.

"It wasn't a victory, but they said I did a decent job," he said.

Sometimes that is all you can do. It is the calculus of warfare. Eason, Plumstead, and Scappiticci had told him as much. Following graduation, each had taken tours in Afghanistan, and each was continuing Erz's education. The long, gray line was a brotherhood, after all, and lessons were made to be passed along. But the biggest lesson, they told him, could be learned only firsthand.

"At the end of the day, if all your guys are alive, it's a hugely rewarding experience," Erz said. "And you want to feel like that every day you are out there."

One year from now. Eighteen months. Soon enough, Erz would meet that challenge in some faraway field of strife. His family, his soldiers, and his country were betting that his forty-seven months at West Point would have prepared him to be his best in the worst possible situations.

# 3

"You have ninety seconds to say good-bye."
—Cadet Nathan McVey, June 27, 2011

They descended upon Eisenhower Hall Theatre at first light, "cadet candidates," teenagers with mussed-up hair—young men in T-shirts and jeans and young women in shorts or slacks and polo shirts. Their parents and siblings trailed along, in awe of West Point's granite chapels, the morning light shimmering off the river below them, and the statues of famous generals standing sentinel and breathing history into every corner of this stately campus. Above Eisenhower Hall Theatre, Trophy Point was crowded with the families and would-be Plebes gazing out to a breathtaking view of the Hudson River Valley, one that had become synonymous with the United States Military Academy and had been rendered in famous paintings and photographs since the early nineteenth century. The captured artillery from the Revolutionary War to the Spanish-American War was spread like furniture across the lawn—iron cannons, chipped shells, and even a loop of the Great Chain that had once stretched across the river and made the Hudson impassable for the British as America sought its independence.

Smack in the middle stood Battle Monument, a column of polished granite that reached forty-six feet high and split the blue sky. The cannons at its base are inscribed with the names of 2,230 Union officers and soldiers who died in the Civil War. The great American architect Stanford White designed it, and the surviving officers and soldiers of the Army paid for it with a monthly contribution that ranged from a dollar for enlisted men to twenty-seven dollars for a major general. On June 15, 1864, Major General George B. McClellan stood at the proposed site of the Battle Monument and offered words that the cadet candidates heading to Eisenhower Hall 147 years later may not yet have fully understood, but their parents certainly had: "The poetry, the histories, the orations of antiquity, all resound with the clang of arms. They dwell rather upon the rough deeds of war than the gentle acts of peace."

Behind them a statue of George Washington on horseback fronted Washington Hall, the mess hall where the cadets would eat at least some of their three squares, and on the rocks above it the Cadet Chapel jutted out and etched a formidable Gothic skyline.

No one could blame the parents for their swelled chests and teary eyes. Mile-wide grins and red-rimmed eyes were the rule here today. This was West Point. If their sons and daughters were willing and able, they would spend the next forty-seven months of their lives learning exactly what duty, honor, and country meant at a time when the United States was at war.

It was Reception Day, or R-Day, and 1,250 cadet candidates were about to embark on their long journey to becoming Army officers. This day was intended to obliterate their past lives and begin the process of rebuilding their bodies, minds, hearts, and souls from the ground up. It had begun at 6:00 a.m. sharp, with groups of two dozen or so cadet candidates being herded into Ike, as Eisenhower Hall was known, where they were welcomed briefly by a member of West Point's military command and then by an upperclass cadet. Each read from an anodyne script welcoming them to the Academy and offering, in the briefest details, what would await them in the coming hours.

"You're about to take your first steps into becoming a leader of character, an Army officer, and a member of the long, gray line," said Lieutenant Colonel Todd Messitt.

The presentation took all of four minutes and ended with an almost chilling pronouncement that sent the cadet candidates scrambling and took their parents' breath away.

"You have ninety seconds to say good-bye," Cadet Nathan McVey told them.

Larry Dixon stepped into the aisle and let his fellow cadet candidates go to their folks. He watched the tight embraces and family group hugs as he made his way to the side door, where the red-sashed cadets waited to begin the long, grueling process that would turn them into Plebes. Larry was here alone because his mother, Laura Ashley, understood better than most the path her youngest child was heading down. She raised Larry and his two older sisters, Karisha and Shakira, while serving twenty-four years in the Navy, rising to the rank of chief petty officer. West Point was a long way from their home in Bremerton, Washington, and Larry's mom and sisters chose to come in the fall for a long parents' weekend rather than the short and jolting handoff here on R-Day. Besides, Larry was as prepared as he was ever going to be: Laura ran the proverbial tight ship at home, instilling rules and discipline.

Larry had had a further taste of military life the previous year while attending the United States Military Academy Prep

School. His arrival at West Point was one of the most eagerly anticipated by Coach Ellerson and his staff not only because of his football prowess but because Larry Dixon was the kind of outstanding individual they wanted to fill their football program with. He carried himself with a gravity beyond his nineteen years.

Larry was an A student with a diverse résumé, and he had already demonstrated that he was a natural leader. At Olympic High School, he had been a three-time All–Washington State selection as a halfback, and the West Sound's all-time leading rusher with 5,182 yards and fifty-nine rushing touchdowns. He had been a two-time team captain in football as well as in basketball, where he played point guard. And in track and field, Larry won far more than he lost in the 100-meter dash, and he finished third in the state in the shotput. Larry was accomplished, fast, and powerful. And yet he failed to generate interest from the University of Washington or other programs in the Pacific-10. He was also overlooked by colleges in the Mountain West and Western Athletic Conferences.

The reason was clear: Larry was short—perhaps reaching five foot ten on his tiptoes. He was stout as well, tipping the scales at 230 pounds. Larry was not a can't-miss thoroughbred for a big-time college factory, but he was the perfect service academy prospect: tough, malleable, and versatile on the field. Coach Ellerson and his staff had already switched dozens of players' positions over the past two seasons. They did not need to switch Larry over to defense or do anything too drastic, just move him up in the backfield to fullback, where his power and smarts would make him a dangerous first option in Army's triple option and wishbone sets.

Better than that, however, Larry had the trio of intangibles that would serve him far beyond the football field: character, intellect, and ability. It was the nonnegotiable checklist for Army football under Coach Ellerson. Bring enough Larry Dixons to West Point and the Black Knights would win for years to come—and the Army itself would benefit.

Larry was the model recruit for what everyone hoped would be a long and prosperous Ellerson era. He had the grades and the talent to come straight to West Point, but Ellerson intended to take advantage of the academy's prep school whenever possible. Why not ease a young man into the demands of military life? Why not give him a year to mature physically and emotionally? He could develop proper study habits and understand Army's special brand of discipline. He could also get a head start learning the intricacies of the triple-option offense and the double-eagle flex defense. Every other major college football program can redshirt freshmen, holding them out of competition but not practice so they can gain maturity without burning a year of eligibility. At West Point and the other service academies, redshirting was not allowed. Coach Ellerson could, however, refer recruits to the United States Military Academy Prep School for a fifth year of high school and a season of higher-level football and have it paid for by the federal government.

The night before R-Day, at a picnic for Army's fifty-five football recruits and their families, Larry's charisma lit up the whole backyard. He possessed a lighthouse smile, and a year at the Academy's prep school had embedded the "sirs" and "ma'ams" in his conversation. He was easily the leader among the thirty football players coming here from the prep school. Larry knew their parents and worked the backyard assuredly. He also made it a point to introduce himself to the other true freshmen—the ones coming straight from high school—wandering around with if not exactly a frightened look in their eyes at least an overwhelmed expression.

Steve Erzinger and a couple of other Firsties were on hand as well and offered handshakes and smiles to their new teammates. Larry was one of the few who took advantage of their presence, approaching Erz and asking what advice he might have for him and the other cadet candidates as they entered Cadet Basic Training. Erz passed on the wisdom of his mentor General White: "Don't be a hero and don't be a goat."

As Larry Dixon and the other cadet candidates pushed through the side doors of Ike Hall, it was clear to them that they were all goats for the foreseeable future. They were herded into a corridor to board the school bus that would take them to Thayer Hall to begin processing.

"Eyes forward, hands cupped, move with purpose"—the command pierced the still morning as one cadet, then another, and another, leaned into the lines of wide-eyed candidates inching toward the buses.

Nearby, Cadet Angela Smith explained what was behind the treatment of the would-be Plebes for the next twelve hours, the next six weeks, and the coming year. She was the regimental commander, or "Queen of Beast," in charge of a 270-cadet cadre, and she was going to put them through their paces in these key opening weeks when they would be sleep-deprived, physically challenged, and, ultimately, rudely awakened to the life of high standards and hardship they had chosen. Like every other cadet, Smith had once stood where this bunch was now.

"It hits you when you get the ninety-seconds call," she said. "It's unnerving. The first impression is always the greatest. We want to be role models, not demeaners. So we want to create stress through high standards but not necessarily stress through any sort of embarrassment. You want them to have that R-Day experience that they can talk about later on, because it's part of the West Point camaraderie, an experience shared by all cadets."

Before Larry and his classmates were placed fully at Smith's mercy, they were raced through Thayer Hall, where their wardrobes and sundries were rebuilt from the ground up as well. Cadets come here empty-handed but don't stay that way for long. Larry filled his Academy-issued duffel bag with eighteen pair of briefs, eighteen white crewneck T-shirts, two athletic supports, one pair of epaulets, six white short-sleeve shirts, four pair of athletic shorts, twelve pair of athletic socks, one reflective belt, one bathrobe, one rain cover for a hat, one pair of cuff links, and two dozen other categories of items that fall into clothing and uniform accessories.

His parade gear encompassed four white waist belts, two breastplates, six pair of white gloves, one tin of brass cleaner, and another half dozen plates and pockets. His field gear ran twenty-six categories long and included everything from a rifle set, two canteens, rappelling gloves, foot powder, rucksack, and knee pads. Larry was issued two mattress covers, one pillow, two sleeping bags, and a gray blanket. The same precision was applied to sundries as cadet candidates were given four bars of soap, one tube of shampoo, one glass tumbler, a clipboard, two combination locks, black shoe polish, and so much more. Mom and Dad were gone but not forgotten as the cadets got a box of stationery, a book of stamps, and one package of ballpoint pens.

Larry had little to worry about at the West Point barbershop—he had always worn his hair close cropped. But he could not beat back a huge smile at the sight of twenty barbers, clippers in full hum, buzzing hair off the cadet candidates in bunches. So far, fourteen pounds of hair had been swept up and weighed, according to a whiteboard on the wall. It was still early—at R-Day in 2010 forty pounds were collected. The record for the longest-haired cadet candidate class, according to West Point barbershop lore, was seventy-nine pounds and was set in 1979.

When Larry stepped into a classroom on the fourth floor of Thayer Hall, two military lawyers—captains—were waiting. They were there to administer the cadet oath to this group of twenty cadet candidates. Larry was anxious and eager, and his mind was racing as he edged into a desk. On the desktop was a laminated card and the Agreement to Serve. On the card was the Cadet Honor Code, an elegant distillation of what character meant here at the United States Military Academy.

"A cadet will not lie, cheat, steal, or tolerate those who do," it read on one side.

If that wasn't clear enough, the other side offered "The Three Rules of Thumb."

1. Does this action attempt to deceive anyone or allow anyone to be deceived?
2. Does this action gain or allow gain of a privilege or advantage to which I or someone else would not otherwise be entitled?
3. Would I be unsatisfied by the outcome if I were on the receiving end of this action?

The United States Military Academy fixed its moral compass clearly and simply. Once the two lawyers were assured that everyone understood what was expected, they asked the cadet candidates to stand and raise their right hands to recite the oath. Ten hours from now, at 6:00 p.m., all 1,250 of them would take the oath on the Plain before the reviewing stands filled with their families. That was for show. This was the real thing.

Larry breathed deep, kept his eyes straight ahead, and joined his fellow cadet candidates in the oath.

"I, Larry Dixon, do solemnly swear," he said, "that I will support the Constitution of the United States, and bear true allegiance to the National Government; that I will maintain and defend the sovereignty of the United States, paramount to any and all allegiance, sovereignty, or fealty I may owe to any State or Country whatsoever; and that I will at all times obey the legal orders of my superior officers, and the Uniform Code of Military Justice."

It was done. Larry and his fellow cadet candidates were told to quickly change into their gym shorts and T-shirts. Unlike Clark Kent, they came out of the bathroom as anything but superheroes. Larry was ready to meet the red sashes and surrender his life to West Point's Corps of Cadets. He was marched through the stone archways by a platoon sergeant and squad leaders he'd soon know way too well, but now he was helpless to remember their names. It was pushing one hundred degrees, and the new cadets were soaked through their newly issued T-shirts and gym shorts. They looked even worse in their knee-high black socks and Oxford low-quarter dress shoes. The courtyard smelled like the suntan lotion that had been slathered on the white domes of the newly shorn cadets. At least the female cadets looked something like themselves—they had kept their hair. Most unfortunate of all were the new cadets who required eyeglasses: each was issued oversized tortoiseshell-framed windshields with a band fastened to the back of the head, commonly referred to as birth control glasses "because no one got laid in them."

"Right turn, march."

"Eyes front."

"Parade rest."

"At ease."

Commands ricocheted around the courtyard as the cadre leaders put the new cadets through the most basic of drills. Larry did what every other new cadet did when not being drummed by the cadre: he held the New Cadet Handbook in front of his eyes and started memorizing the more than one hundred pages of military knowledge he was expected to spit back on command and verbatim over the next six weeks and beyond. This first week alone he needed to absorb rank and insignias, pay grades, weapon postures, rules of saluting, division patches, uniform differences between officers and enlisted, and West Point's definition of a leader of character.

"A leader of character seeks to discover the truth, decide what is right, and demonstrate the courage and commitment to act accordingly, sir," Larry said.

"Do I look like a sir to you?" growled a female cadet.

"No, ma'am."

On the second steps of the barracks stood four cadets calling out in their own rhythm and time, "Step up to my line, not on my line, not over my line." Below them was a taped line that might as well have been strung with electricity.

Each of them was the "Cadet in the Red Sash"—the first cadre member a new cadet needed to report to in order to join his or her company. On a board nearby was the script the new cadet needed to follow.

"Sir, New Cadet [Name] reports to the Cadet in the Red Sash for the first time as ordered."

One after another of Larry's classmates was being berated and sent back to the line. They had stuttered or saluted weakly or stepped on the line or did nothing at all but be a new cadet.

"Step up to my line, not on my line, not over my line," sing-songed the cadet on the step before Larry.

He rushed forward, dropped his duffel bag, gave his best West Point salute: fingers together and extended in a straight line, arm parallel to the ground, palm angled toward his eyes.

"Sir, New Cadet Dixon reports to the Cadet in the Red Sash for the first time as ordered," he said.

The red sash looked him up and down and then growled, "Move out, New Cadet." Larry picked up his bag and ran inside to find his room and join Delta Company.


Back inside Ike Hall, the parents and families of the members of the United States Military Academy's class of 2015 heard from Lieutenant General David H. Huntoon, West Point's fifty-eighth superintendent. He had arrived here the previous summer from the Pentagon, where he had been director of the Army Staff. Huntoon was a 1973 West Point graduate, and he had attended the academy at the same time as General David Petraeus, the commander of U.S. forces in Afghanistan. Huntoon had been an executive officer to the chief of staff of the U.S. Army, senior officer for Operation Just Cause, deputy director of plans for Operations Desert Shield and Desert Storm, and deputy director of plans in the Eighteenth Airborne Corps.

He stood ramrod straight and talked easily, without a script, about how grateful the Army—and the country—was to them for delivering the best and the brightest here. Make no mistake, he told them, their sons and daughters were the best and the brightest. Above the stage, a PowerPoint slide painted an extraordinary portrait of the class of 2015. There had been 13,954 applicants to West Point, and 4,344 young men and women had received the required nomination from a member of Congress. Some 2,554 of that group had been deemed academically rigorous and physically fit enough for the United States Military Academy, and of these, 1,249 had been admitted. The incoming class included 97 high school valedictorians, 122 class presidents, and 704 team captains. All told, they had accounted for 1,090 varsity letters.

The general let these facts and figures sink in. He let the gasps fill the auditorium and gave some space to the tears rolling down the cheeks of the moms and dads. He then told them of the great things their children were going to accomplish over the next forty-seven months and promised that he and every officer posted here would take the greatest care of them. He was a parent, too, after all. In fact, only a month earlier he had watched his son Stewart graduate from West Point. "As proud and as good as you feel right now," he told them, "wait until how you feel then."

Two hours later, Larry Dixon and his classmates marched onto the Plain for the oath ceremony. The 1,249 individuals who had shuffled onto the post twelve hours earlier wore the summer white-over-gray uniform with white gloves. They stepped at 120 beats a minute and made their about-faces as if they had been practicing all their lives. Many of their parents scanned the crowd with cameras, trying frantically to pick out their sons and daughters from the sea of buzzed heads and crisp uniforms.

What a difference a day had made.

# 4

"It isn't that coming to football is less difficult or challenging than the other things we do here. It's just that it is the most fun thing we do. It just brings us the most joy."

—Max Jenkins, August 1, 2011

There is perhaps no team in college football that is happier to start preseason training camp than the Army Black Knights, and it showed in their broad smiles and exuberant dance steps as they got off the school buses that had hauled them up from the barracks to the Kimsey Athletic Center and filed into the locker room for practice. Two and half hours here on the practice field was nothing compared to the rainy nights of maneuvers at Camp Buckner or the suffocating days of field training at Fort Benning that they had done earlier in the summer. Breaking down stunting defenses or spread offenses on film beat the hell out of calculus and chemistry.

Besides, this was the one place no one was a Cow or a Yuk, a Firstie or a Plebe, but simply teammates playing the game that had brought them to West Point in the first place.

There were photographs to be taken, reporters to talk to, and a game one month away to dream about.

Max Jenkins and Trent Steelman, the two quarterbacks, had come to the football complex early. Behind them, the Lusk Reservoir rose and fell gently in the summer breeze. Before them Michie Stadium, nestled amid trees and cliffs, welcomed them back for another season. Max and Trent stepped onto the field, looked at the empty seats, and grinned.

"It isn't that coming to football is less difficult or challenging than the other things we do here," said Max. "It's just that it is the most fun thing we do. It just brings us the most joy."

Trent Steelman was the starting quarterback and as close to a true football star as Army had. He looked the part, too. He was built like a wrestler, a ripped two hundred pounds, and had an "aw shucks" grin that perfectly matched his western Kentucky drawl. On the field, however, Trent was fierce and raw-boned and seemed to compete perpetually angry. He was, sort of. Despite leading the Bowling Green Purples to three consecutive state high school championship games and a combined 50–7 record, he was recruited by only one Division I school—Army. Trent had been a regular at the Vanderbilt summer football camps and had hoped to earn a scholarship there, but the offer never came. Kansas asked him to walk on, as did Western Kentucky, his hometown university. Trent, however, wanted to be wanted, so he signed with the Black Knights and went to the United States Military Academy Prep School first, to determine whether he was truly Army material.

Coach Ellerson had inherited him when he arrived in 2009 and was glad he did. He named Trent his starter a week before the opening of his inaugural season, making Trent only the seventeenth Plebe to start at quarterback for the Black Knights and only the seventh since 1951. Heading into this, his Cow season, Trent had started twenty-five consecutive games as quarterback and was bearing down on the Academy record of thirty straight games behind center, compiled by Leamon Hall from 1975 to 1977. Trent had led the Black Knights to that 7–6 record and bowl victory over SMU the previous season, but he still was a work in progress. He was coming off shoulder surgery, and his confidence had been badly shaken by a fumble on the goal line against Navy that was returned ninety-nine yards for a touchdown and perhaps cost Army its first victory over its rival in nine years.

Trent needed to mature, perhaps more off the field than on it. He had been an uneasy cadet since arriving at the U.S. Military Academy Prep School in 2008. He was caught with a cell phone talking to his girlfriend during a surprise room inspection just two weeks into the school year and was horrified when the infraction resulted in punishment for all three hundred members of the school. Trent was the fourth-string quarterback and miserable. He called his father, Bob, and said he wanted to come home. Bob Steelman would not let him.

Trent stuck it out, but his struggle with West Point life was ongoing. He needed, and was benefiting from, the countless hours he spent with his backup, Max Jenkins.

Max was a Firstie, and this was his last season of football at West Point. Max was going places in the Army if he wanted to, a prospect that frankly dismayed him. He had recently been named the brigade deputy commander, the second-highest leadership position in the Corps of Cadets. He had risen to the position by being smart, outgoing, and a near-perfect cadet. Max had started the summer as summer garrison commander in charge at times of up to sixteen hundred cadets who came through West Point for training or en route to somewhere else. He then spent the second part of the summer in Wiesbaden,

Germany, with the Army Corps of Engineers, where he was a program manager and part of a team trying to build a hospital. Max was a thinker and was intrigued by the political savvy and diplomacy necessary to put together $1.2 billion of building projects in a foreign country. He had always thought that he would select infantry as his Army branch, the preferred destination for the best and the brightest at West Point. Infantry, after all, was the warrior class, the tip of the spear. After Wiesbaden, however, the Army Corps of Engineers was in the running.

Max had come to West Point almost on a whim, committing here on his official recruiting visit, which also was the first time he had set foot on campus. He didn't know anything about the United States Military Academy, really, until then. In high school, Max had been a member of the National Honor Society as well as the Fellowship of Christian Athletes and YMCA Teen Corps. In all ways, his was the kind of résumé that shows up on the superintendent's PowerPoint on R-Day. He had heard of Generals MacArthur and Bradley and Patton and was duly impressed by West Point's history and picture-postcard beauty. But he was more wowed by the weight room and the massive hangar-sized indoor practice center. Like Trent and Erz and his more than one hundred teammates, the message he heard loudest was that Army offered a chance to play Division I football.

It didn't matter that he'd be one of ten quarterbacks on the roster or that Army football wasn't truly suited for a pure passer like Max. He once threw for 589 yards and eight touchdowns in a game to set the single-game school record at Langham Creek High School in Houston, Texas. Max was invited to walk on at a couple of Big 12 schools and was actively courted by the Ivy League. Instead, he came here. At first, he didn't really prosper, but he endured in a way that drew the attention of West Point's tactical officers—TACs—the officers in charge of mentoring and developing the next generation of leaders. He struggled through Plebe year and thought about transferring like everyone else, but he never conveyed that to his fellow Corps members or his teammates. In fact, Max was always the first guy to offer encouragement or extra help to the "goat," or fellow Plebe, having the toughest time.

Football was another story; he was merely lost. Max appeared in a single football game as a freshman. It was a home game against Louisiana Tech, where his brother, Ross, was the starting quarterback. The previous Army coaching staff thought it would be neat to have the brothers on the same field at the same time. Unfortunately, it came on the game's final snap, when Max took the deep back position in Army's "victory" formation and watched one of the other ten quarterbacks take a knee to end the game. It wasn't the sort of debut Max had in mind.

When Rich Ellerson was hired at the end of the 2008 season, Max did what came naturally to him: he prepared. He went online and found out everything there was to know about Ellerson, then amassed information and studied Cal Poly's triple-option offense. At the first practices, Ellerson recognized how focused Max was each day at practice and how his teammates gravitated toward him. Still, he was not as athletically gifted as Trent, a freshman, or as experienced as Chip Bowden, who had held the quarterback job in 2008. Max made the most of his limited practice snaps, however, absorbing the nuances of Ellerson's triple option better than the quarterbacks ahead of him. He didn't get behind center in a game during his sophomore season, either, but he refused to get discouraged.

Max appeared in a game, however, for a single snap just as

he had as a freshman, but this one was way more gratifying. Against Duke, Max was a late substitute on the kickoff team. He scrambled downfield and made his first and last career tackle.

The following spring, his father, Mark Jenkins, suffered a fatal heart attack. Max was driving home from spring break in South Padre Island when he heard the news. His dad had had an enlarged heart, a condition that had gone undetected for forty-eight years. Mark Jenkins had been home alone. Max's mom, Felicia, was in St. Louis with his sister, Regan, for a volleyball tournament. When a day had passed and she had uncharacteristically not heard from Mark, she called a neighbor and sent him over to check on her husband. The neighbor found Mark dead on the kitchen floor. Mark had coached many of Max's teams growing up. He had paced the fence along the first-base line of Little League stadiums and stalked and hollered from the sidelines of middle school football games to the point that Felicia refused to let him sit with her. Neither Mark nor Felicia had ties to West Point, but they were thrilled with Max's decision and understood that—football or not—he had a chance to profoundly change his life.

Max had every excuse, and more than an impulse, to walk away from West Point after his father's death. Instead, he chose to double down. That summer he was platoon sergeant at Beast Barracks and caught the attention of Major Scott Hequembourg. Everyone at West Point has heard what others haven't and committed themselves to life as a military officer, or they wouldn't be up each morning at 6:30 a.m. and slogging through woods all summer. Major Hequembourg recognized something deeper in Max: he was reflective and looking for a better way to lead his life. Major Hequembourg had wrestled at West Point and, after three tours of Iraq, could see when leading came naturally to a cadet. He watched as Max gently moved from the hard-case cadets who couldn't make their way through a uniform inspection to the supermotivated Plebes as easily as he dealt with the high command. On the road marches, Max always led from the front. His subordinates always had their equipment squared away. They all liked Max and followed him enthusiastically. Most impressive was how he dealt with his fellow Yearlings.

"He had compassion," Hequembourg said. "He didn't display the harshness other cadets often do. It's difficult to lead your own peers, to make them do something they don't want to do."

When Cadet Basic Training was over, Major Hequembourg, along with Sergeant Normand Paquin, his noncommisioned TAC, asked Max to pursue a key leadership position in the Corps.

"They saw some sort of potential in me," Max said. "I thought they were crazy at first, but they were right. I guess I was looking for something."

Hequembourg and Paquin wanted him to pursue the position of battalion sergeant major, one of the three top jobs for a Cow. Hequembourg knew the time constraints on athletes, but he urged Max to push himself. He told him that there were times that he might have to miss a practice or football meeting, but he sensed that Max cared about more things than where he stood on the depth chart. Hequembourg also told Max that he wouldn't get any better coasting through his final two years. Max not only accepted the challenge but performed magnificently enough that when Major Hequembourg and his colleagues sat down to choose the cadets to fill the top leadership positions, his name was near the top of the list.

. . .

Andrew Rodriguez had a hard time making his way to the locker. Every couple of steps, he was stopped for a hug, a pat on the back, or a fist bump and all manner of other hardy "welcome backs." His popularity on the team rivaled Max's, and as thrilled as his teammates were to see the man they called "A-Rod" back in the football center, they were surprised as well. Andrew was not supposed to be here after missing the entire previous season with a back injury that had threatened to derail his military career. And for Andrew not to be able to continue on what all expected to be a brilliant military career would have been a tragedy.

His father, David Rodriguez, is a four-star general who is in charge of the U.S. Army Forces Command after commanding the Eighty-second Airborne and forces in Afghanistan. General Rodriguez had played defensive end at West Point from 1972 to 1975. Whenever Andrew was asked if his father was a four-star Army football letterman, he didn't miss a beat.

"It depends who you are talking to," he said with a knowing chuckle. He had heard the legend of David Rodriguez's playing prowess around the kitchen table only to later find out there had been some liberties taken by the teller.

Andrew was the youngest of David and Ginny Rodriguez's four children. The oldest was his sister, Captain Amy Rodriguez ('06), who was in Iraq working as a medical services officer. Melissa was an elementary school teacher and David, just two years older than Andrew at twenty-four, worked as a contractor in the Navy Yard in Washington, D.C. Andrew and his siblings had mostly grown up at Fort Benning and, for his high school years, in Alexandria, Virginia. He said that his childhood was like that of anyone who grew up in a multichild, multisports-playing suburban household with carloads of kids and sports equipment passing in the night and dinners eaten on the run. David and Ginny Rodriguez made sure at least one parent was at each game or performance, and if that meant the general showed up in uniform, so be it.

There had been plenty of doubt over whether Andrew was going to follow Amy and his father into the family business. He had plenty of options coming out of Bishop Ireton High School, where he split time between running back and linebacker, was a two-time captain, and led the team to a second-place finish in the Virginia Independent League. He was a member of the Washington Post All-Metro Second Team and had earned letters in basketball, lacrosse, and track and field. He was courted by all the Ivy League schools but had settled on Princeton as the right one for him.

But Andrew could not walk away from West Point, whose previous coaching staff had recruited him and with whose history and lore he was intimately familiar. He insisted that neither his father nor his mother or sister pushed him. They didn't have to—the place had been a part of his entire life. Andrew liked the Academy's structure. He wanted to be a part of the football team's renaissance, and, yes, Andrew wanted to be like his dad.

The smart money already was on him having a military career every bit as decorated as his father's. It was a life that he knew and loved despite the long family separations that he had endured while his father was away being General Rodriguez. He knew war's consequences and saw it often when he visited injured soldiers at Walter Reed Army Medical Center, where he had volunteered as a high school student.

Andrew was wicked smart—he carried a 4.14 grade point average as a mechanical engineering major and ranked third in a class of 1,052 cadets. He had posted twenty-one A-plus grades and recorded six terms with a GPA of 4.0 or higher. He was polished in all facets of cadet life—the summer after his sophomore year, he distinguished himself in infantry training at Fort Benning and completed academic leadership training in Vicenza, Italy. He could play some football, too. He had been Army's leading tackler as a sophomore. He was fast, explosive, and had a head for the game.

All of this had been put in jeopardy, however, one afternoon the previous summer, in an off-season workout. He was just warming up and barely had any weight on the bar when he felt a twitch in his back. Andrew stopped and tried stretching gently, when, as if he were engulfed by a giant claw, he was overcome with paralyzing spasms. He had herniated two disks, which was unfortunate but addressable. Soon, however, the diagnosis got worse and the prognosis turned dire: doctors discovered that Andrew had been born with a narrowing spinal column, a condition that put pressure on his nerve endings. The condition, called spinal stenosis, was painful and had eventually ended the careers of Washington Redskins offensive tackle Chris Samuels and safety Darryl Morrison.

Forget football. Andrew was worried about his career in the military. The infantry had little room for a weak-backed, pain-wracked officer, no matter his pedigree or how brilliant his intellectual talents. Andrew needed two spinal surgeries, and his doctors suggested that if he wanted to give his recuperation the best chance to succeed, then he should not return to West Point for the second semester of his junior year. David Rodriguez was in Afghanistan, but Ginny was at Fort Myer, the U.S. Army post next to Arlington National Cemetery, across the Potomac River from Washington, D.C. So Andrew moved home.

But it was important for Andrew to graduate in May with

his class. The Firsties may not have been the most talented
class to grace Army football, but they were a smart, cohesive
group. Max Jenkins, Steve Erzinger, Brad Kelly, Austin Barr—
Andrew ticked off all their names and memories of weekends
in New York City and the houses upstate that they had rented
together with dates to celebrate the milestone moments at West
Point, such as the 500th Night Ball.

To make sure that he could share Ring Weekend, Branch
Night, and 100th Night with his friends, Andrew took two
online courses from West Point in the spring. He picked up
another course over the summer and had just signed on to take
an unthinkable twenty-four hours during the fall semester, following it with twenty-two more in the spring. The previous
spring at home had been lonely and isolated as Andrew did his
schoolwork, worked out in the modest gym on post at Fort
Myer, and hung out with his mother.

Coach Ellerson had encouraged Andrew to rebuild his
body, telling him that he was not going to be allowed to play
again without assurances from his doctors that he would not
be risking further damage by playing football. During spring
practice, Ellerson thought there was no way in hell that A-Rod
was coming back and, frankly, was deeply worried that he
might not be able to continue in the Army. But here he was at
preseason camp with the approval of his doctors.

In fact, Andrew might have been more surprised than anyone else that he was here. He had stuck with his arduous rehab
schedule—at least three hours a day, often more—but had
resigned himself to missing his last season at West Point. He just
wanted to stay in the Army, especially after spending six weeks
of the summer as a platoon leader working with the Yearlings
in training at Camp Buckner. It was where he was supposed to
be. Commanding soldiers was what he wanted to do.

As the summer was winding down, the doctors put Andrew through sets of progressive exercises in an attempt to determine exactly how much his back could handle. Each spine and vertebrae structure is different, as is each person's threshold for pain and uncertainty. Just days before camp was to start in August, Andrew's doctors told him that he could give football a try. No one knew for sure if he was ready to deliver, or take, a hit. In fact, Coach Ellerson resolved to go slowly and kept A-Rod out of contact drills for as long as he could.

It took several weeks, but one day at practice, Coach Ellerson told Andrew to remove the blue jersey worn by the injured players, that it was time to see what he could do. They both had to know whether Andrew's back was better and whether his heart was still in football—and there was no better place than in an open field tackle drill to take the measure of both. Andrew lined up across from Jared Hassin, the Black Knights' bruising 230-pound fullback. Andrew barely had gotten his chinstrap on and did not have time to be afraid or even to think about what was going to happen.

Jared charged. Andrew ducked and drove, and they met in the middle in a violent collision, Jared getting his shoulders and waist over him. No one on the practice field moved. Jared got up tentatively and reached a hand down. Andrew bounced up, smiling ever so slightly. The collision had been good for his soul. For the Black Knights as well—there were whoops and cheers and clapping for the teammate they had clearly missed.

It didn't matter whether A-Rod would remain in pads or had to wear street clothes, his teammates were glad he was back, especially the younger players—the Ellerson recruits—whose initial exposure to Army football had been in the company of Andrew and Max and Steve Erzinger. They had been the guys who had looked the recruits in the eyes and told them how tough the military life was, and how challenging the academics were, and how miserable Plebe life would be for them. They also told them that despite all those obstacles the recruits would thrive at West Point just like the older players had. Andrew, Max, and Steve had promised them something else as well: someday when they were Firsties, they would feel like their senior teammates did now and would not have traded their time at West Point for any other college experience.

Andrew, Max, and Steve had made quite an impression on the young Black Knights. So much so that they lobbied Coach Ellerson to change the way the team picked its team captains. In the past, Army had rotated game captains during the first half of the season before selecting permanent captains midyear. This edition of the Black Knights wanted to select Max and A-Rod now to join Steve Erzinger as its captains. Coach Ellerson thought over his team's request and agreed to break protocol and name Max and A-Rod captains from the outset of camp. In fact, the more he thought about it, the more encouraged he was about the progress of his program.

"They've seen Max and A-Rod do a few things besides practice football," Coach Ellerson said. "Those two have taken a few extra laps around here. Erz, all three of them, are so complete. They're out between the white lines making plays; they're in the huddle; they're on the sideline; they're in the Corps; they're in the classroom. There are no holes in that leadership group."

# 5

———————

"I sat there and looked out the window and thought, 'I don't know if I can be here. I don't know if I can do this.'"

—Larry Dixon, August 8, 2011

Two weeks into Beast Barracks, Larry Dixon was ready—no, desperate—for it to be over. He was just surviving the 5:00 a.m. wake-up calls and predawn wind sprints and push-ups. He was jumpy from the nonstop questions and corrections and reminders from cadre members about the many areas in which he had been found wanting. Larry had embraced the "suck," as the interminable marches were known, his legs clicking off the 120 beats per minute and swiveling into turns on their own while from the waist up his arms and chest were heavy from exhaustion and his head foggy and swimming with too much information. He was ready with answers from the CBT handbook when, out of nowhere, a cadre member demanded to know: "Who was Dennis Michie?"

"He was a member of the class of 1892 and the captain of the Army football team," Larry said, trying not to stammer.

"First Lieutenant Michie was killed in action in San Juan, Cuba, in July 1898."

"Recite the phonetic alphabet," ordered another.

"Alpha, Bravo, Charlie, Delta," Larry answered, rolling on all the way through "Zulu."

He knew his branch badges by sight: two crossed rifles for infantry, crossed field guns for field artillery, and for armor a front view of an M26 Pershing tank, gun slightly raised, super-imposed on two crossed cavalry sabers in scabbards. He had the Army company, division, and mottoes down as well: A Company, First Cavalry Division, "First Team"; E Company, Eighty-second Airborne Division, "All American"; Regimental Headquarters, the 101st Airborne, "Rendezvous with Destiny."

Larry had his West Point history down cold, too. He knew that the church organ in the Cadet Chapel boasted 18,700 pipes and was the third largest in the world, and he knew that Benedict Arnold's plaque was in the old Cadet Chapel. It held only his rank and date of birth—Arnold's name and the date of his death had been gouged out. He could tell you that Peter Townsend constructed the Great Chain in the Stirling Iron Works, twenty-five miles southwest of West Point in Warwick, New York. There were approximately twelve hundred links, each of which weighed between 90 and 120 pounds. The chain was stapled onto large logs and floated to reach from Chain Cove to Constitution Island. The point was to stop British ships so artillery could be rained on them from the batteries of West Point and Constitution Island. He knew the Corps legend and lore.

"When did the Corps stand to arms?"

"In the New York riots against the draft of 1863, word reached West Point that a mob was going to visit and burn the Academy. Ball cartridges were issued to the cadets. Pickets of cadets with a field gun at each point were established at North and South Docks and Gee's Point. No attack was made, however."

Larry Dixon could smile and even dream a little about football and the faraway game with Navy when cadre members, knowing he was a Black Knight, demanded "Slum and Gravy."

He sang.

*Sons of slum and gravy,*
*Will you let the Navy*
*Take from us a victory? Hell no!*
*Hear a warrior's chorus,*
*Sweep that line before us,*
*Carry on the victory! Let's go!*
*Onward! Onward! Charge against the foe,*
*Forward! Forward! The Army banners go!*
*Sons of Mars and Thunder,*
*Rip that line asunder,*
*Carry on to victory.*

Larry was able to recite an excerpt from the famous speech that General Douglas MacArthur delivered on May 12, 1962, upon his receipt of the Sylvanus Thayer Award for outstanding service to the nation. Even in Larry's current distressed state, MacArthur's words offered him encouragement. They inspired him and gave him shivers.

"Duty, honor, country: Those three hallowed words reverently dictate what you ought to be, what you can be, what you will be," MacArthur said, in his final address to the Corps of Cadets. "They are your rallying points: to build courage when courage seems to fail, to regain faith when there seems to be little cause for faith, to create hope when hope becomes forlorn."

Still, a little more than two weeks into Beast, MacArthur's words were not enough to rouse Larry from a deep funk. He wanted to quit. They were breaking him down. He told his mom so on the phone. It was the first time he had heard her voice in weeks, and the words just rushed out. He was so tired, so defeated, that he couldn't muster any energy, couldn't keep his dark thoughts at bay.

"I sat there and looked out the window and thought, 'I don't know if I can be here,'" he said. "'I don't know if I can do this.'"

Mom wouldn't have any of it. Instead, she answered as Chief Petty Officer Ashley would and as she had previously when she oversaw young sailors. Larry thought she even sounded bored.

"If you don't like it, come home," she said. "Someday you're going to have soldiers depending on you. You need one hundred percent motivation and effort now so they will be able to count on you then. It's not going to be easy, and you can't be worrying about yourself."

Larry knew she was right. Up at the Kimsey Center, Coach Ellerson and his staff would have been surprised to hear that Larry was struggling. The word they were getting was that the kid was a natural—that he was handling Beast with grace and helping others pull through. But Ed Mullen, a classmate from the USMA prep school, recognized Larry's confusion. He pulled him aside one night at dinner and told him to take it one day at a time and not to take it personally. They were trying to break him.

Beast, indeed, does a good job of weeding out the noncommitted. It seemed to Larry a day didn't go by without news of a cadet throwing in the towel and going home. In fact, their names were announced to the upperclassmen training at Camp

Buckner. No one took joy in it, but it was a reminder to all cadets of what was expected of them. There also had been a tragedy during Beast Barracks. Cadet Jacob Bower was found dead in the woods during a land navigational exercise. He had been a three-sport athlete and valedictorian at East Fairmont High School in Fairmont, West Virginia. Like many of his classmates, Bower had set his sights on West Point as a young boy. He had spent the past year in the weight room, running with a loaded backpack, and was by all appearances in tip-top shape. Now, however, U.S. Military Academy officials were investigating how an apparently healthy eighteen-year-old had died during Cadet Basic Training.

It was another blow to Larry's psyche. Between his mother and Ed Mullen, however, Larry dug deep and found the grit to hang on one day at a time. The physical stuff was a breeze. Each cadet has to do at least forty-two push-ups in two minutes. Larry more than doubled that with eighty-seven. He was safely above the fifty-three sit-ups minimum, too, with sixty-one in two minutes. He was fast and fit enough to complete the two-mile run in 14:02, well below the 15:54 cutoff, though he was hurting afterward. Larry preferred running in short bursts and knocking people over. He had enjoyed a good time on the seventy-five-foot rope rappel, slinging down the face of a cliff feeling like Spider-Man. The tear gas chamber was another story. Beneath the mask, Larry had to fight off claustrophobia while he felt the entire liquid contents of his chest and head empty out.

Larry still saw himself as a kid and liked feeling that way. He never felt like less than one, however, than he did when learning how to use the tools of his trade: the weaponry. He was a deadeye shot with his M4 assault rifle. Larry even found inner peace in the ritual of maintaining his M4, how the organizing of the small-arms swabs and pipe cleaners, the chamber, bore, and toothbrushes gave way to the clicks and catches of bolt and pin. He could work his way through the scales of hand grenades from the AN-M14 incendiary, to the ANM-8 HC white smoke for signaling, to the M61 and M67 for killing enemy soldiers. Larry wasn't sure what to make of the enormity he felt working on these skills with live rounds. He knew he wasn't playing toy soldiers anymore.

Larry's biggest challenge was to master map and navigational skills. His military map often looked like Sanskrit to him. He was clumsy with a protractor and a compass. Grids, points of elevations, and terrain characteristics left him befuddled. In short, Larry was the kind of guy who got lost in the woods, which is not what you want in the Hudson Highlands. His greatest frustration during Beast was getting lost and disoriented and then having to walk for hours when all he wanted was to go home and go to bed. That, in turn, resulted in cadre members jumping all over him at the mistake, causing another, and another, so "you feel like you're screwing everybody up."

It took Larry six weeks to figure out that, yes, he was screwing up his fellow Plebes, and they him, but that was one of the points of Beast.

"You had to dig down," he said, on the verge of March Back, the twelve-mile "suck" from Camp Buckner back to West Point. "It takes grit, true grit to get through the day. You've got to have high performance every day because somebody's life might depend on it."

In the end, Larry made it through training. He still had the march to negotiate, with forty pounds of stuff in his rucksack and scorching temperatures broiling him and his fellow Plebes. The class of 2015 was now a smaller group than the one that had started on R-Day—thirty-two of them had decided on a different path and had gone home. The class of 2015 still had plenty of company, though, as more than one hundred former graduates had come back to join them, including a large contingent from the class of 1965. Each new class is paired with their predecessors from fifty years earlier. This was the first of the milestone events that they had pledged to attend throughout the cadets' four years. They were part resource and part reminder that the long, gray line is real.

Coach Ellerson was there, too. He also made the whole march back. You cannot preach stacking Ws without showing your players how it is done.

Family members and Army officers lined parts of the route offering high fives and congratulations to Larry and his classmates. At West Point, there are only three parades held specifically for each class. Larry had the first one on R-Day behind him. The second was to be in five days on Acceptance Day, or A-Day, where he and his classmates would wear their white hats as official members of the Corps of Cadets. The third, of course, was going to have to be earned over the next forty-five months, along with a diploma and the gold bars of a second lieutenant.

Larry didn't want to think about that right now.

• PART TWO •

# YEARLING YEAR

# 6

"What a bold mold of rolled gold! What a cool jewel you got from your school!"

—West Point Plebes, August 19, 2011

The cannon fired a blank charge across the Academy grounds, the report echoing up the hill to Michie Stadium. It was 5:00 p.m. and time for the American flag to be lowered on the Plain. The nightly rite of retreat is a moment when time stands still at West Point. The cars along the roadways stopped. The cadets and Army officers on foot turned and saluted. The Black Knights stopped what they were doing and did the same. Classes had resumed, and football season was two weeks away.

After just a week in the classroom, Steve Erzinger was already buried with homework and reading assignments. It was time to bear down again, and Erz was trying to get in gear one final time. It was hard to do at the beginning of the school year. Home leave had taken him out of the West Point state of mind, and preseason training camp was not a grind at all—playing and preparing for football four hours a day was a joy when there was no homework and you could go to bed clearheaded and at an early hour. Steve had done so up until the previous weekend.

Now he was tired, but he hardly regretted it. The previous weekend the Firsties had received their class rings, and Steve's girlfriend, Danielle Hansen, had come up from Nashville, Tennessee, for the celebration and a night out in New York City. Danielle was a senior at Lipscomb University in Nashville, where she was studying nursing. She was a member of the tennis team and had earned the ironic nickname "Diesel," in contrast to her blond hair and willowy 110-pound frame. It had been a memorable weekend and Steve was in high spirits. Their courtship had had a difficult beginning and, as is often the case in the romance rituals of West Point cadets, required plenty of initiative and even more patience.

The United States Military Academy is a hard place to do much of anything fun, so finding Miss (and, yes, Mr.) Right takes planning and effort. In fact, it could keep some of the military's finest minds busy for weeks strategizing at the Army War College in Carlisle, Pennsylvania.

Women have been part of cadet life since 1976, when the first 119 of them enrolled as Plebes, and some thirty-five years later women make up roughly 20 percent of the Corps of Cadets and hold many of the key leadership positions. The rules of romance, however, are still rudimentary. There are essentially three paths to enjoying the company of the opposite sex. First is what is often referred to as "cadating," or asking out a fellow cadet. There are inherent challenges to overcome here, especially for men, beginning with the odds that, at four men to one woman, are overwhelmingly not in their favor. There is the fact of life that cadets at West Point already live in close quarters—if not in a fishbowl—and there is nowhere to escape from your classmates. Beyond those limitations, as well as the shared duties of being a soldier, most cadets feel that cadating lacks some essential magic.

The "Two Percent Club" offers a narrow if not altogether realistic alternative to companionship with the opposite sex. It is the name (as well as success rate) for those cadets who show up for Reception Day with hometown sweethearts and actually leave West Point as a second lieutenant with the same significant other in tow.

Dear John and Dear Jane letters are written and received in landslide proportions by Plebe and Yearling cadets. Among the contributing factors to those long odds that are not seen at other colleges is the sheer time commitment of being a cadet and the lack of privileges to go home on weekends or to have much more than three weeks off at a time. And finally, military life is difficult in the best of times and harrowing during times of war, as hundreds of thousands of families can attest in the past decade as their spouses have been sent to Iraq and Afghanistan.

Erz met Danielle the way most West Point cadets do—through a friend, another cadet named Kristina Keltner. The previous January, Steve was looking for a date to the 500th Night ball, which commemorates the days left until graduation. He had exhausted his list of likely candidates from his hometown of Houston and was looking to be adventurous. He asked Kristina if she had any friends who might like to go on a blind date at West Point. She suggested Danielle, a childhood friend of hers from Zionsville, Indiana. Steve called Danielle and asked if he could buy her a plane ticket to come to the ball. It was in the thick of tennis season, however, and she had to decline.

Still something sparked over the phone. They spoke easily to each other. Steve kept asking her out. Danielle kept answering that she was not available.

"That was pretty much the story of the semester," he said. "We always had some sort of conflict with our schedules."

Soon, however, the phone calls grew longer and they came later at night as a friendship developed. Finally, in May, Steve decided that he had to meet this girl in person. Term End Exams, or TEEs, as they are known at West Point, were approaching, and they were followed by a leave. Steve decided to head south. One of his friends was graduating from the University of the South in Sewanee, Tennessee, so he used that as cover.

"The plan was to spend time with her, and if it didn't work out, then I could just claim I was going to my friend's graduation at Sewanee outside of Nashville," he said. "Things with her went really well. We agreed to meet again, and I went to my buddy's graduation. It ended up being the best of both worlds."

He had been with Danielle on every break since. The Ring Weekend festivities had been her first visit to West Point, and Steve had pulled out all the stops. They had stayed at the Palace Hotel after dinner and took a tour of the city on a yacht. Danielle, however, had been more impressed by West Point itself. She thought it was one of the most beautiful places on earth and could not get enough of its history and the fact that so many other customs had sprung from it.

The tradition of class rings at American colleges and universities, for one, is believed to have originated with members of the United States Military Academy's class of 1835. Inside the Jefferson Hall library, Danielle saw the rings of deceased former graduates, including those of some of the most famous alumni—Generals Douglas MacArthur ('03), Dwight D. Eisenhower ('15), and Omar Bradley ('15).

It was the ring ceremony itself that had moved Danielle more than any of the razzle-dazzle of New York. It was brief, magisterial, and solemn. She watched from about three hundred feet away as Steve stood at attention with the other Firsties at Trophy Point. The cadets glistened and looked like princes in their India white uniforms.

"We recognize that each West Point ring tells the story of the wearer's deepest sense of achievement, of the eternal values of the academy and the bond of unity which binds each graduate and West Point," said Father Edson Wood, a Catholic priest and brigade chaplain, in his invocation.

Each Firstie had custom designed his or her ring the previous year. Steve went for simple elegance: his was a solid gold band with the United States Military Academy's crest and a diamond in the middle.

He was proud of his ring. He did not run once from the Plebes, who, in a more lighthearted tradition, were allowed the rare privilege of chasing down Firsties to recite what was known as the ring poop. It was a corny rite, but over the years ring poop had been sung to some of the greatest military leaders in American history. Some Firsties made a game of eluding the Plebes, tearing through campus and leaping over walls. Not Steve. A gaggle of them caught him beneath an archway as he headed to his barracks.

"Oh my God, sir, what a beautiful ring!" they sang. "What a crass mass of brass and glass! What a bold mold of rolled gold! What a cool jewel you got from your school! See how it sparkles and shines? It must have cost you a fortune! May I touch it, may I touch it please, sir?"

# 7

"I got blown up by an IED in Afghanistan. I stepped on it, and lost both my legs. My guys, when I got blown up, they were there. I had a squad leader holding my head. Everyone was tourniquetting my legs, getting me together. They were getting me a bird and getting me out of there."

—Lieutenant Tyson Quink, September 2, 2011

It was Tuesday afternoon, and Major Chad Bagley was in overdrive. The Black Knights' season opener against Northern Illinois was five days away, and Army's director of football operations was in perpetual motion. He was the team's military coordinator, which was as vital to Army football as Coach Ellerson's offensive and defensive coordinators. "Major Bags," as most called him, was the person who made sure that each of the more than 130 players was at the right place for the right training in the summer; he helped schedule their classes and physical tests. It was no small feat puzzling together how to integrate a little bit of football into the cadets' military and academic duties without adding to the already taxing stress level.

Major Bags was one part life coach, one part scheduler,

another part travel agent, and always mentor and role model. His influence cut both ways. He was the guy who took Coach Ellerson's hopes and dreams that were scrawled on the War Room's whiteboard and turned them into an efficient operation. He was the one who unscrambled the alphabets of CBT, CLDT, and CFT and was able to group the linemen at Fort Benning and get strength coaches to them, as well as turn a shed at Camp Buckner into a makeshift weight room where Trent and other Cows and Yuks lifted each morning at 5:00 a.m. Major Bags also made sure the coach and his staff understood cadet life and which of their players were cut out for it and which ones needed prodding or a little more understanding.

On his mind at the moment was getting the Army eighteen-wheeler loaded with two tons of equipment and on the road for the twenty-four-hour trip to DeKalb, Illinois, well ahead of the 737 he had chartered for the coaches, players, band members, cheerleaders, officers, and assorted alumni and boosters who altogether numbered a party of 180. Hotel rooms at the Hilton Lisle Naperville had been booked, meals arranged, and police escorts secured for their buses as soon as they landed at O'Hare and throughout their travels in northern Illinois. Major Bags had Army's itinerary, from the team's departure at 1300 Friday, September 2, 2011, to its 0350 arrival back at West Point on Sunday, September 4, 2011, reduced to an index-size card that he had laminated and handed out to everyone on the trip. It was strategy—planning and logistics streamlined and passed on with economy. It is what West Point officers did and part of the reason America wins wars.

Major Bagley was like many of the Army officers at West Point—hyperefficient and unfailingly polite. His hair was brushed with gray, though he was just thirty-eight and had a round boyish face. He spoke softly, listened hard, and looked

you in the eye as if your eyes were diamonds and he was trying to determine their exact cut and clarity. He had the bearing most West Point officers had, the kind that said, "I lead;
you follow." Bagley had graduated from West Point in 1995
as a three-year varsity letterman and, as a senior, the captain
of the Army golf team. He preferred his camouflage battle
fatigues and beret during the workday but put a polo shirt
and some Bobby Jones slacks on him and he'd look at home
at any Professional Golf Association tour event. In fact, the
previous spring, he had filled in as Army's interim golf coach.

He had served in the field artillery and was an accomplished
officer, with tours served at Fort Drum in New York and Fort
Stewart in Georgia, before returning to West Point to become a
tactical officer and regimental executive officer in the Academy's brigade tactical department. It was a choice assignment
that was hard to get and went only to the most promising officers. The TAC teams were the legal commanders of the Corps of
Cadets and created and maintained the command climate. Their
members conducted the reviews, oversaw operations, and were
the hands-on instructors for all things military. They did their
fair share of problem solving and romance advising, but their
most important task was to identify cadets with the same passion and commitment they possessed and to show them the
rewards and the nobility of being a career Army officer.

They did this by living, breathing, and oozing duty, honor,
country and by explaining the dividends that military service
paid. It was a job Bagley and his fellow TACs cherished. Their
offices were right in the barracks and they really felt—no,
knew—that they were having an impact on the lives of cadets.
They fell somewhere between fancy guidance counselors and
all-knowing Yodas for the next generation of Army officers. At
West Point, there is a lot of talk about character and being a

laboratory for leadership. Bagley believed it deep in his soul. He knew West Point was profoundly different than any other assignment in the Army. It was the one place where officers were not judged wholly on performance.

"When you're out on a mission, failure is not an option," he said. "When something goes wrong for a cadet here, no one gets shot or no one dies. We're here to make sure the cadet learns from his failure or responds to the situation differently the next time."

The opportunity to pursue a graduate degree was one of the perks of becoming a West Point TAC. Bagley had earned a master's in counseling and leader development from Long Island University. He had experienced adventure and polished his craft at Air Assault School, had taken Field Artillery Officer Basic Course, and attended Armor Captains Career Course and Combined Arms and Services Staff School. He also spent a six-month tour in Iraq as an operations officer in the Sadr City section of Baghdad, where he helped the Army Corps of Engineers build a water treatment plan in the midst of mortar and sniper attacks by members of Muqtada al-Sadr's Mahdi Army.

Over the past decade, the Army has retained about 51 percent of its West Point graduates beyond their five-year commitment. Bagley was one of the 36 percent of his class who had stayed on ten years and one of the 29 percent who had served fifteen. He intends on being one of the 27 percent of West Point graduates to stay twenty years, which is retirement age, or beyond. He doesn't blame his classmates or any other West Point officers for taking their "five and fly," the line for those who opt out as soon as the five-year military commitment is satisfied. With two wars under way in Afghanistan and Iraq, after all, not many families were built for frequent deployments into perilous situations. The private sector is alluring, too, with its promises of big money and the opportunity to create and innovate. Military officers are in demand for a reason. According to a 2006 Korn/Ferry International study, male military officers are almost three times as likely as other American men to become CEOs. Pete Dawkins ('58) was chairman and CEO of Primerica. James Kimsey ('62) was the founding chairman of America Online and in 1996 was named the company's chairman emeritus. He was the lead donor for the 117,000-square-foot building that held Bagley's office directly above the Black Knights' locker room, a sports medicine center, a weight and cardiovascular fitness room, and a swimming pool.

Bagley loved West Point and being an Army officer, and he was perfectly content with military life. He was in his sixth season with the football program and his second as director of operations. He lived on post with his wife, Susan, and their three children: his thirteen-year-old son, William, his eleven-year-old son, Andrew, and his six-year-old daughter, Anne. He didn't want to go anywhere, especially now when Army football was on the rise. He had just been approved for promotion to lieutenant colonel, however, and there was always a possibility it could come with a new assignment.

Bagley knew his football and had come by it honestly as a boy growing up in South Carolina, worshipping all things Clemson. (His dad, Sack, a retired teacher, is a spotter for the Tigers' radio broadcast team.) Now, however, the Tigers were his second-favorite team. He was an obsessive follower of college football on the Internet through ESPN and Twitter and newspapers. He knew which teams could play and who could be had.

He knew most of all that the Black Knights were in deep this year and that the first half of the season was going to make or break them. Bagley sounded like he belonged on ESPN's

*SportsCenter* when he ticked off the strengths and weaknesses of this edition of Army football at a recent lunch—except for the "Mr. Joe's" that dotted his scouting report. Between his military manners and Southern upbringing, he couldn't make himself call civilian acquaintances and colleagues by their first names.

"We were eighth in the nation in rushing last year, and we have Trent and five other starters back," he began. "We're talented at the skill positions: Jared Hassin, our fullback, ran for a thousand yards last season and gained them in bunches. Our biggest loss was at slot back with Pat Mealy graduating. Malcolm Brown started last year and is back, and Raymond Maples played a lot last year as a Plebe. We're replacing the whole line, but we'll be okay. We're going to move the ball, but the problem is if we're going to be able to stop anyone."

Bagley grimaced and leaned back in his chair.

"We're not very big on the defensive line," said. "We're going to have to play a lot of young guys, and that's never good. To win here, you need seniors. By the time you are a Firstie, you have figured things out, how to manage your time, how to maintain your studies. You're a finished product. You understand the sacrifices you've made and appreciate how far you have come. You want to have fun and appreciate what West Point is, and to begin to look forward a little to what's ahead."

He shrugged and then smiled.

"We're in tough, especially with all the expectations after last season," he said. "The only thing I can promise is that we'll play hard."


Army football is about tradition, and Coach Ellerson saw some traditions that had evolved haphazardly and decided to institutionalize them. One grew out of the fact that each year at the Navy game, each player wore a patch of his division in the Army, reflecting their potential assignments after graduation. The coach liked the tradition. He thought it was the kind of connection he wanted his team to have with their fellow cadets as well as with the troops. So he took it a step farther: he had the whole team wear the patch of a specific Army division on the uniforms each Saturday. Better, he asked the seniors to write to the division commanders and invite a speaker who would come to address the Black Knights on Tuesdays after practices. For the opener, against Northern Illinois, the Firsties chose the patch of the First Infantry Division, the "Big Red One."

This was the same choice the 2009 and 2010 teams had made, and each time it had led to opening season victories. Max Jenkins and Kingsley Ehie gave the briefing on the patch as well as the speaker, Lieutenant Colonel John Vermeesch.

The Big Red One is headquartered at Fort Riley, Kansas, and traces its roots to 1917, when General John "Black Jack" Pershing arrived in France with the first American Expeditionary Force. The Big Red One has fought in both world wars, Vietnam, Operation Desert Storm, Bosnia, Kosovo, Operation Iraqi Freedom, and Afghanistan.

Lieutenant Colonel Vermeesch was one of the more popular officers in Brigade Command. He was currently the regimental TAC officer for the Third Regiment and had a reputation as a "hooah" leader who projected strength, confidence, and high morale. "Hooah" is an Army call and response that echoes around West Point mostly in the summers during military operations. It is shorthand roughly for: "I'm a warrior. I'm ready. I serve America every day, all the way."

It fit Vermeesch well. He was a 1990 graduate of West

Point and had a chest full of medals and badges, including the Bronze Star with oak leaf cluster, the Purple Heart, and the Meritorious Service Medal with oak leaf cluster. He had served in Desert Storm and had done several tours in Iraq, the most recent as the commander of First Battalion, Eighteenth Infantry Regiment in northwest Baghdad. In January 2005, when he was stationed in Sadr City, however, a letter he wrote to friends and family went viral on the Internet. He was writing about the first free Election Day in Iraq.

"Today may be the proudest I have ever been of being an American soldier," he wrote. "As I walked the streets of Sadr City today, I saw the best the human spirit has to offer." He did not gloss over how difficult it was to arrive at that milestone or the high price that the Americans, as well as Iraqis, were still paying. He talked about suicide bombers and a rocket attack in his sector and how it killed four individuals near a polling station, including a child. "Despite that, the people cleaned up the mess and continued to flood into the polling center to vote," he wrote. "While neighborhood members mopped the blood into the gutter, others continued to enter the station to take advantage of their newfound freedom. The mother of the dead child voted, despite her grief."

Vermeesch wrote of the strange but warm feeling of walking the same streets where he had narrowly escaped with his life the previous fall and where he was now being thanked by Iraqis. It was the first time, he confessed, that he had felt the whole war had been worth it. "It absolutely convinced me that David Heath, Brandon Titus, Henry Risner, Yoe Aneiros, David Waters, Mark Stubenhofer, and the over 1000 others did not die in vain," he wrote. "It convinced me that SGT Mendoza lost both of his legs in the pursuit of a higher purpose. I am assured that the 91 soldiers from this task force who have bled in the streets of this city did so in order to make this day a reality."

He wrote movingly about the ink on the fingers of the proud Iraqis who had voted. Neither he nor his soldiers really thought this day would ever come. "As I type this I am nearly brought to tears by the pride I feel for the flag that adorns my right sleeve, and for all that it stands for," he concluded. "God bless you all, God bless the seeds of freedom, and God Bless America!"

Vermeesch hit many of the same themes with the players after practice and did so in rapturous and fiery fashion. He was "hooah" and as he laced his sermon on duty and sacrifice with well-timed profanities, he reinforced the belief in his—their—cause so the Black Knights' hearts lifted and their spirits soared. Vermeesch told them they were special and guaranteed them that nobody in Division I football did what they did—not Northern Illinois or Northwestern or any of their opponents, not even Air Force or Navy.

"While you guys were doing CBT, CFT, and CLDT," he said, "they were all sitting on the couch this summer playing a video game of what you guys actually were doing out there in the field."

The players were roaring by the time Vermeesch handed over a football emblazoned with the Big Red One's logo and all the previous fields of battle it had graced. He kept the football on his desk. He told them to write the final score of the Northern Illinois game on it the following Monday. Win or lose, he would be proud to have it back.

They stood at attention, hats cradled in their left hands, as the team captains walked the ranks of their teammates for a uniform inspection. Max handled the offense and A-Rod the defense. Each fussed with epaulets, made sure the brass in the hats was polished to a high gleam, circled behind to see if the haircuts were up to snuff, and then back in front to make sure faces were shaved smooth. The Black Knights damn sure were expected to look like perfect United States Military Academy cadets when they left on a road trip. When the football team traveled, it represented the Academy, and the high command understood that first impressions matter. The Plain behind them was empty, and three buses idled and groaned beside them waiting to take them to Stewart International Airport in Newburgh, New York, where a charter was set to take them to the great state of Illinois. It was 1320, and the laminated itinerary Major Bags had prepared called for a 1330 departure from West Point.

Coach Ellerson was waiting across the road at Battle Monument in another nod to Army tradition. In the 1940s and 1950s, Coach Red Blaik had gathered his Army teams here at Trophy Point on the Friday before each game. He thought it was the appropriate place to offer wise words or quiet thoughts before Army set off to find glory at places like Notre Dame and Rutgers and the University of Pennsylvania. Coach Ellerson had revived the tradition, and this afternoon he turned this moment over to a guest speaker.

Beside the coach in a wheelchair was Tyson Quink, and behind Tyson was his wife, Tera. They had met five years earlier when Tyson was a six-foot-three-inch, 280-pound offensive lineman at West Point and Tera was the football team's first female head manager, a coveted position previously held by such celebrated cadets as Douglas MacArthur, the future astronaut Frank Borman, and the future national security adviser Brent Scowcroft. Tyson and Tera were in their dress uniforms with their red berets pulled low after just coming from the funeral of a classmate—First Lieutenant Timothy J. Steele, who had died in the Kandahar province of Afghanistan. Steele was the fourth member of the class of 2009 to die and the eighty-fourth graduate of West Point to lose his life since September 11, 2001, in support of the missions in Afghanistan and in Iraq.

Tyson had lost both legs below his knees in Afghanistan the previous spring. He had stepped on an improvised explosive device. When the first member of his squad reached him and asked where his tourniquet was, Tyson pointed to a medical pouch strapped to one of his severed legs several yards away from his body. He also suffered a traumatic brain injury, which was still showing itself with lapses in his short-term memory. Tyson had undergone fourteen surgeries and had been bombarded with a variety of painkillers and antibiotics. He had been fitted for one prosthetic leg and was waiting on another.

The couple was living at Walter Reed National Military Medical Center in Bethesda, Maryland, where Tyson was learning to live with a pair of steel shins and feet. Both Tyson and Tera looked exhausted and much older than their twenty-four years. In an instant, what had been a very simple life plan had been violently waylaid in a faraway country. All Tyson had wanted to do was earn a command, serve his time, and perhaps go home to his native California.

"Maybe be a teacher and coach some high school football, and live with my dog and my wife, and have some kids," he said.

Neither Tyson nor Tera had given up on that dream, but there was a whole lot of hard work and uncertainty awaiting them. They were soldiering on and gratefully so. Steele's funeral was only their latest reminder of what might have been. When Coach Ellerson asked Tyson to speak to the Black Knights, he said yes. He had not played for Ellerson but had treasured his days on the Army football team. He didn't know exactly what he was going to tell the team, either. He remembered the sheltered life of a cadet and how he had felt then that death or a life-changing injury was something that could happen only to someone else, anyone else but him.

Tyson now knew better. There was no amount of CBT, CFT, or CLDT to prepare anyone for being in the wrong place at the wrong time in a hostile place like Afghanistan.

As the team crossed the road and fanned out on Battle Monument, the steely military gaze the cadets usually fall back on in uncomfortable situations began to soften, especially among the Firsties. They had been on the team when Tyson played and Tera ran the practice operations and patrolled the sidelines during games. Erz, Max, A-Rod, and the rest of their class gravitated toward the couple, offering nods and taps to their shoulders. Coach Ellerson got right to the introductions.

"This is the moment we stop and reflect that we are part of a brotherhood," the coach said, "an extended brotherhood, a long gray line, of all those who came before, and all those who come later. Some of you know Tyson and Tera, Army football, class of 2009."

Tyson Quink looked up from his chair, scanned the semicircle before him, and took a deep breath.

"I got blown up by an IED in Afghanistan," he said haltingly.

"I stepped on it and lost both my legs. My guys, when I got blown up, they were there. I had a squad leader holding my head. Everyone was tourniquetting my legs, getting me together. They were getting me a bird and getting me out of there."

Tyson paused. His voice was close to cracking.

"Those guys I'll never forget—I see their faces all the time," he said. "It's important what they did. They would have done it because it was their jobs, but they did it because they didn't want to lose someone they were tight with. Me and my platoon sergeant slept together. We practically held hands we were that close."

Tyson was tearing up, as was Tera. Coach Ellerson was shaken, and virtually all the eyes of the Black Knights were wet and glistening. Tyson breathed deep and dug up a hint of a smile and the memory of a time when he was not in a wheelchair and missing part of his legs, a time when he was at West Point, and not for a funeral. He wanted them to understand that brotherhood is at the heart of the Corps of Cadets. It was how the long, gray line was sustained from generation to generation. What he did not wish on any of them was the brotherhood that was forged in combat and around heartbreak and lost limbs. Tyson's platoon had suffered heavy casualties. His medic had stepped on an IED and lost his leg a week after Tyson. The sergeant who had held Tyson's hand at night had gotten blown up and injured as well a few weeks later.

They all had remained in touch, but Tyson made it clear that he wished it was under different circumstances.

"When I got here, that kind of brotherhood I found was football," he said. "These guys, you'll stay in contact with them forever. You guys stay close. It will help you on the field."

His voice then dropped to a whisper.

"It will help you when you're a lieutenant."

# 8

UPON THE FIELDS OF FRIENDLY STRIFE
ARE SOWN THE SEEDS THAT,
UPON OTHER FIELDS, ON OTHER DAYS,
WILL BEAR THE FRUITS OF VICTORY.

—General Douglas MacArthur

Lieutenant Colonel Vermeesch's Big Red One football was returned with a disappointing score written on its side: Northern Illinois 49, Army 26. Army's season started ominously when both teams were kept in their locker rooms for an hour as a thunderstorm rolled through, making an electric jigsaw puzzle of the midwestern sky. There was talk of canceling the game altogether, but the storm eventually cleared, and after an abbreviated warm-up and delayed kickoff the show, indeed, went on. Coach Ellerson and the Army faithful wished it hadn't.

Northern Illinois wasted little time, forcing the Black Knights into a three and out on the game's first possession. Things quickly deteriorated from there as the Huskies blocked Army's punt. It was the first career punt for Kolin Walk, and Northern Illinois recovered and returned the ball sixteen yards for a touchdown. The season was just one minute and seventeen seconds old and the Black Knights were down 7–0. From there, Northern Illinois did not waste much time. Five of the Huskies' six touchdown drives lasted two minutes, forty seconds or less. The sixth was a ninety-seven-yard march in the third quarter.

There were not many positives to take away from the game. Trent Steelman ran for just 37 yards on seventeen carries and completed five of eleven passes for 86 yards. He also didn't look like a quarterback making his twenty-sixth consecutive start at Army or running the triple option: he threw an interception and had trouble holding on to the ball, losing a fumble inside Northern Illinois's 5-yard line as the first half was coming to an end. The defense was taken apart by Northern Illinois quarterback Chandler Harnish, who threw for 195 yards and five scores, and ran for another 80 yards and a touchdown. Army also lost its best and most experienced lineman for the season when Jarrett Mackey was caught crossways in a block and injured his knee in the first half.

Jarrett had started all thirteen games the previous season and had worked hard in the summer at Fort Benning to marble his 240-pound frame with muscle. His time in Georgia had also given Jarrett focus. He had shadowed some Rangers, the troops that get the most training and are considered the Army's elite members. He had sampled Ranger School and proved to himself that he had more than the right stuff to succeed in its ranks. Jarrett was going to become a Ranger. He was physically fit, mentally tough, and had located his inner "Hooah." Jarrett had had a great summer and returned to West Point a cadet at peace with his decision to serve. He was in the best shape of his life and was looking forward to returning to another bowl game.

Now, however, Jarrett looked heartbroken as he watched

the rest of the game with his leg up, knee wrapped, and his mother, Myrna, at his side. Someday soon, Myrna Mackey might well be on the verge of tears awaiting word from Jarrett in some faraway battle zone. This night, however, it was her tender pats and soothing words that kept her twenty-one-year-old son's tears to a trickle.

Max Jenkins entered the game in the fourth quarter to mop up, and he threw an eleven-yard touchdown pass, the first of his career at Army. In limited time, A-Rod had three tackles. It was a start. Andrew was back on the field but a couple steps slower and perhaps ever so tentative. He was rusty after more than a year away from the game.

Steve Erzinger, on the other hand, had hurtled around the field for a career high of twenty-one tackles, including three and a half for a loss, which tied his career high. Mainly, his gaudy statistics showed how poorly the rest of the defense had played.

It was a sullen, solemn, and sore flight home for the Black Knights, and when they arrived back at Stewart International Airport at 0350 John Mumford, Army's defensive ends coach, watched as Jarrett on crutches led a parade of ice-pack-toting, stiff-legged, bruised, defeated, and sleepy-eyed teammates across the tarmac to the buses. Hardest hit was the defensive line. Parker Whitten was on crutches and defensive ends Clayton Keller and Colin Linkul also could not finish the game.

"It looks like Gettysburg," he said.


Any other day, it took Coach Ellerson three minutes tops to descend from his third-floor office and cross Mills Road to the stone bridge over the Lusk Reservoir to his brick Georgian home on Partridge Place, which had been built by Red Blaik on what was then called Snob Hill. This afternoon it took nearly thirty minutes and could have dragged on longer if there hadn't been a practice to conduct. Coach Ellerson and his staff had watched the game film from Northern Illinois for the last forty-eight hours and were frustrated and disturbed. They saw their players out of position in basic sets, defensive backs crossing their feet like junior high schoolers, and an assortment of missed tackles, weak blocks, and turnovers. Worst of all, however, was his team's lack of energy.

It agitated the coach, and when he got agitated, he'd pace and talk, then stop talking, then pace some more, getting even more agitated the whole time. He was a big man, six foot three, with a broad chest and busy hands. He flexed them often and shook them loose at the wrist. He was a stalker on the practice field and sidelines and moved with a cross and swivel stride reminiscent of John Wayne. He swooped into one group and was out just as fast and on to another. He was not a screamer or given to profanities. He was a hands-on teacher who lined up across from the defensive linemen for a series of wrist grips, forearm shivers, and hand-to-hand combat to get past blocks. He had distilled the techniques from martial arts books. He was a tactician, demonstrating the new no-huddle offense he had installed to his triple-option offense. Coach Ellerson also was a historian of Army football.

He was fascinated, as are all hard-core Army football buffs, by the relationship between Blaik and General Douglas MacArthur. He could tick off the facts of their relationship chapter and verse, including how Blaik had first met MacArthur in 1919 when the would-be coach was merely a Firstie and the thirty-eight-year-old brigadier general had just become the youngest superintendent in the history of the Academy. They were at a formal reception when MacArthur offered

Blaik and his classmates a warm handshake and followed that up by offering them cigarettes. Everyone knew that smoking was prohibited for West Point cadets, but MacArthur, already a war hero for his exploits in World War I, wanted them to know he was a regular guy. It was the beginning of a lifelong friendship and mutual admiration society between a legendary football coach nicknamed for his auburn hair and the general known as "Dauntless Doug." Both were proud of the association. Throughout Blaik's eighteen years as Army's head coach, from 1941 to 1958, a portrait of MacArthur in full salute hung behind the coach's desk.

The general liked football and football players, having been a decent athlete himself. MacArthur was a good-glove, weak-hitting outfielder for the Army baseball team as a member of the class of 1903. With barely 130 pounds stretched on a five-foot-eleven-inch frame, Cadet MacArthur was too small for football, though he did share in the team's camaraderie as its head manager in 1902.

But life at West Point was not all fun and games for MacArthur, as he suffered through a particularly trying Plebe year. His chief tormentors were cadets resentful of his Army pedigree. His father, Lieutenant General Arthur MacArthur, had been awarded the Congressional Medal of Honor for his service in the Civil War, and he was the military governor-general of the American-occupied Philippines at the time, a tenure that ended a year later due to clashes with the civilian governor, the future president William Howard Taft. Douglas was also mocked because his mother, Pinky, had accompanied him to West Point and had moved into a suite at Craney's Hotel, which overlooked the grounds and where she would stay for the next four years. This proved to be a toxic combination for MacArthur as well as for another of his classmates with a military lineage and a doting mother staying at the hotel: Ulysses S. Grant III, grandson of the former general and president. MacArthur and Grant were brutalized and humiliated by the Southern cadets who were still mad about what they insisted on calling the War Between the States. In 1901, MacArthur testified before a special Congressional Committee about the physical punishment and mental harrassment he had experienced and witnessed at the United States Military Academy. His experiences, however, hardly slowed him down or dimmed his ardor for West Point: he graduated as the most decorated cadet in Academy history, ranked first in his class academically, and was the highest-ranking cadet in the Corps.

"Next to my family, I love West Point best," MacArthur often said.

Still, hazing remained on his mind when he became superintendent. He appointed a committee of cadets, chaired by Red Blaik, to address the issue, and he embraced its recommendations, which included a ban against "laying hands," or denying food to Plebes.

MacArthur also refused to hide his enthusiasm for Army football. He would carve time out of his schedule on autumn afternoons and stroll over to the Plain—the parade ground that at the time was also Army's practice field. He would stand on the sidelines, his signature riding crop in hand, watching the coaching staff weave among the players as collisions sounded all around them. He liked to buttonhole an assistant and invite him to the superintendent's office for a personal briefing on how the boys were coming together and what to expect on Saturday.

MacArthur had seen how well athletes in the Army's officer corps executed under the direst pressures of the battlefield.

He wasn't the first to embrace football with its violence as a metaphor for war, but he lent the game some poetry when he declared,

> UPON THE FIELDS OF FRIENDLY STRIFE
> ARE SOWN THE SEEDS THAT,
> UPON OTHER FIELDS, ON OTHER DAYS,
> WILL BEAR THE FRUITS OF VICTORY.

MacArthur felt so strongly about this sentiment that he had it carved into the stone portals of the Cadet Gymnasium. He believed in sports competition so much that he created a comprehensive intramural program and declared that every cadet was an athlete. With the varsity sports, he saw an opportunity to raise West Point's national profile. Everyone talked sports. The enlisted men he had commanded had looked up to the athletes in the army ranks. Until MacArthur's arrival, Army played all its games at home; the Black Knights left West Point only to play Navy. In 1921, the general sent the cadets to New Haven, Connecticut, where they beat Yale 14–7. He wanted Army to take on the college game's powerhouses and even had plans prepared for a 100,000-seat football stadium on the Hudson's western bank. In 1924, two years after he left, the 16,000-seat Michie Stadium was built on a bluff high over the campus instead of his grand design.

Still, MacArthur had demonstrated that he was Army's No. 1 fan. He created the template that Army football has since been built on. His love of the game and his forty-year friendship with Blaik had also given him an exalted voice in all college football.

"Football has become a symbol of our country's best qualities—courage, stamina, and coordinated efficiency,"

MacArthur told a star-studded crowd at the National Football Foundation, which he helped found, on December 1, 1959, at the Waldorf-Astoria Hotel in New York. "Many even believe in these cynical days of doubt and indecision that through this sport we can best keep alive the spirit of reality and enterprise which has made us great. In all my own long public service, both in war and peace, it is the football men that I found my greatest reliance."

MacArthur's passion for football is celebrated not only each Saturday as the Black Knights take the field but also after the final game of each season, when the MacArthur Trophy is awarded to college football's national champion. It is engraved with another of the general's famous quotes: "There is no substitute for victory."

No one knew this legacy better than Coach Ellerson as he stomped along the stone bridge across Lusk Reservoir. Everything that MacArthur had created, and that Red Blaik and his successor Paul Dietzel had built upon, was about embracing the brotherhood and being an Army officer. Ellerson had taken the previous year's team to Walter Reed Army Medical Center to see soldiers their age recovering from horrible injuries but remaining upbeat and driven to overcome them. He had invited Tyson and Tera Quink to address the current team to remind them what is important, what was at stake.

"We talk about the brotherhood because it's real," he said. "It isn't like these guys come back for reunions or go home in the summers and drink beer and hang out at the drive-in with their buddies. Our guys are in awful places doing difficult things."

Ellerson could handle mistakes on the field. In fact, he expected them. This Army team had ninety-four freshmen and sophomores on the roster, and he had put twenty-three players on the field against Northern Illinois who were playing their first snaps of Division I college football.

"Coach Blaik said for every Yearling you start expect a loss," he said. "We've got true freshmen out there, Plebes, who don't know whether they are coming or going in school let alone on the football field."

What had bothered the Army coach the most was the utter lack of joy projected by the Black Knights against the Huskies. His players called him a "hippie coach" because he preached total immersion in the moment. He taught breathing exercises and encouraged the players to find the inner child who sat on the couch playing a video game totally lost and focused on the screen. The Black Knights practiced yoga on Sunday, and it was less about the stretching and more about being in the moment. Ellerson's mantra was a simple one: win the next snap. He wanted his team to play fast and be flexible. Anger over a mistake could manifest itself as tension throughout the body and in slow reactions. Beating yourself up over what happened on the last play brought on tunnel vision and did not allow a player to see the whole field. Be fast. Be flexible. Be in the moment.

He and his coaching staff had to be. They were fishing in a small pond when it came to attracting players who were not only qualified to be accepted into West Point but also might stay and thrive here. The coaches had learned that they could not afford to recruit a kid to a specific position, so instead they put a premium on their potential growth and elasticity. When they looked at high school seniors, they envisioned how they might appear two years down the road without enough sleep after too many late nights in the library and summers spent trudging through the woods and sleeping in tents. Ellerson wanted to see them grow both physically and emotionally before deciding where to play them.

He liked switching players from position to position and turning offensive players into defensive ones and vice versa. He looked at skills and body types—lean and quick could switch between defensive backs, wide receivers, and slotbacks. Brian Cobbs, a Cow, lettered as a Plebe at cornerback, then played slotback as a Yearling, and now was again on defense at cornerback. Big and bruising bodies could become fullbacks, linebackers, or strong safeties, even a quarterback. Kyler Martin, another Cow, had seen action as a linebacker, defensive back, and wide receiver. Wide-bodied, strong, and low-center-of-gravity types were destined to be guards, centers, or nose tackles. Long, strong, and agile were defensive ends to offensive tackles. Chad Littlejohn, a Firstie, had been both a linebacker and a defensive end.

In time, Ellerson knew that he would get the right players in their correct positions. His immediate concern, the one that kept him pacing on the stone bridge, was getting his players' minds right.

"That was as far away from the edge as I've seen a football team in the first game," he said. "We don't like what it says about who we are or how we feel about the game of football. It doesn't come out when you watch the film."

He had sensed that his team was shouldering a load from the success of the previous season. The expectations and desire to achieve an even better record, to earn another bowl game, and to beat Navy were undeniable.

"Whether it built up around the program or when they were back in the company, the modest success last year got everyone excited, and they felt like, 'Oh, boy, there's a lot of expectations, and we are playing really good people,'" Ellerson said. "That doesn't have anything to do with anything. Our job is just to play, go out there, and have fun. We need to drop this rucksack we're carrying around that's weighing us down—the expectations—and relax and play the game."

The previous year Army had put together a season to remember by being mentally tough: the Black Knights ranked third in the nation in turnover ratio, meaning they forced fumbles and interceptions far more than they committed them. It is how a tough, smart, and not awfully talented team wins games—and the proof was right there in Army's record book. Since 2006, Army was 14–4 when winning the turnover battle and just 7–35 when their opponents took better care of the ball. The goal at the beginning of this season was to be number one in the nation in turnover margin, and there was a chart hanging in the Black Knights' locker room intended to track another season where poise and precision carried Army football. After the blocked punt, three fumbles, and interception at Northern Illinois, Coach Ellerson told Major Bags to make sure the chart was removed. The team had moved the ball against the Huskies, gaining a whopping 409 yards on offense, and Ellerson wanted to build on that without distraction. He suspected that this group might be too fragile to see their miscues in black and white. He didn't want it to get in their heads.

With the home opener against a very good San Diego State team just days away, there was not a lot of time to do much renovation on the Black Knights. The Aztecs were perhaps the most physically imposing team Army was likely to see this season. Their previous season's head coach, Brady Hoke, had been an ace recruiter who had turned San Diego State from a 2–10 doormat to a 9–4 Poinsettia Bowl champion. His reward was one of the most coveted jobs in college football—head coach of the University of Michigan.

The Aztecs' current coach, Rocky Long, was a friend and former colleague of Ellerson's who knew how to defend the triple option as well as any coach in the nation. Long had seen it annually from Air Force during the eleven seasons that he was the head coach at the University of New Mexico. He had previously been San Diego State's defensive coordinator and the mastermind that short-circuited Navy's triple option in its 35–14 bowl victory. The Aztecs had opened the season the previous week by waxing Cal Poly, which was still running Ellerson's triple option as well as his double-eagle flex defense, by a score of 49–21.

So San Diego State was more than ready for Army. The Aztecs had a strong-armed senior quarterback, Ryan Lindley, who had thrown for seventy-one touchdowns and 9,740 yards the previous season and was fully capable of picking apart Army's patched-up secondary. San Diego State's sophomore running back Ronnie Hillman had been tenth in the nation in rushing the previous year as a freshman and was assaulting the school records set by Marshall Faulk, a future NFL star and Hall of Famer. Hillman was certain to play on Sundays when his collegiate career was over.

Coach Ellerson knew he had some X's and O's to figure out. Army talent was not enough to beat San Diego State. He needed to get home to the house that Red Blaik built and then back to a team that he fully intended to be part of his Blaik-like football legacy here on the banks of the Hudson. "I'm determined this week to turn off the scoreboard, play the next play, and light our hair on fire—what hair we have—and go after these guys," Ellerson said. "We play hard and fast, on the edge, and let the chips fall where they may. But on the next play, doggone it, 'You are going to get a mouthful from us, pal.' Then, we will see what the scoreboard looks like when that is over."

## 9

"For our generation, it's hard to think of a world where there's not something going on to fight the war on terror. From fifth grade on, it was all about Afghanistan and Iraq. Regardless of what is going on when I graduate, I know it's my mission to serve the country that I have believed in since childhood, and it will be my honor to do so."

—Benn Jebb, September 7, 2011

The sound was forlorn, the tune haunting. Steve Erzinger had heard "Taps" played at 2230 every night he had been on campus for the past thirty-nine months. There were many things he was not going to miss about West Point but listening to "Taps" played each night was something he would. It was supposed to mean lights out, but rare was the cadet who was done with his studies or answering e-mails or simply relaxed enough to shut down and hit the sack. Rarer still was the cadet who was fast asleep before the bugle moaned in the dark. Most of the windows of the barracks glowed into the morning hours as if fireflies were hovering over the Hudson. Still, Erz heard the sound of the bugle and congratulated himself for not only surviving but getting the best of another day at West Point.

In room 531 on the fifth floor of Eisenhower Barracks, Erz
had a book in his lap and much on his mind. He had problem
sets due in his Operations Management and Managerial Finance
classes. He had a project he had to finish for Applied Systems
Design. There was a test in his History of Military Art class the
following week for which he needed to get a jump on the reading. He also had to turn in his choice for the branch of the Army
in which he wanted to serve. Erz was no Douglas MacArthur, or
even a Max Jenkins or Andrew Rodriguez. Max wore a wreath
on his uniform signifying he carried a 3.5 grade point average.
A-Rod had a 4.1 and was ranked third in their class and sported
a bronze star as well as the wreath. Each was certain to receive
his first choice, which was Infantry. It was the textbook route
for West Point's best and brightest. Erz's lackadaisical academic
start as a freshman, however, had finally caught up to him. He
wanted to go to Infantry; it made sense—Erz was a team guy,
and an infantry unit was an awful lot like football—but it was
not a sure thing. And if he did get his choice, he wanted to go to
Ranger School and then to Fort Campbell, Kentucky, with the
101st Airborne Division.

"Success is really based on how well you train your team,
how you practice, and the way you play," he said. "In the field,
if you train and you do all your drills and maneuvers at half
speed and just go through the motions, you're not going to do
it well when you actually have to do it in theater."

Erz was ranked in the middle of his class, and there were
no guarantees that he would get his first choice. There was
only one way for him to take the suspense out of the branch-
ing process and that was by choosing to extend his ADSO, or
Active Duty Service Obligation, an additional three years. In
2005, when the program was in its infancy, cadets called it
"Branch by eBay." For cadets with less-than-stellar grades,

ADSO offered a shortcut to the military career of their choosing. For the Army, it helped boost its retention rate beyond five years and, in theory, built a more experienced officer corps.

Erz was still finding himself. He had no idea what he wanted to do for a career, let alone commit more seriously to the military. He had undergone an academic awakening in the previous two years, though, and he hoped that the Army might recognize it and send him to graduate school.

Erz was not big on deep thinking about life after West Point and the dangers that may be awaiting him as an Army officer. He was hardly alone—one after another of his teammates claimed to worry little about being killed or wounded in combat. One reason was that the United States Military Academy attracted the sort of fearless, committed, and patriotic individuals who presumably knew what they were signing up for. West Point also had a significant population of sons and daughters of military families as well as Academy legacies. This was true of the football team as well. A-Rod was following his father and his sister Amy. Ben Jebb, an offensive lineman, grew up on the grounds; his father, Joel ('82), was a retired major and taught at the Academy's prep school, and his mother, Cindy ('82), was a colonel and the deputy head of the Department of Social Sciences at West Point. Linebacker Justin Trimble was following his brothers, Jeremy ('08) and Jordan ('11). The other reason, of course, that the cadets refused to express fear or consternation about what awaited them was that they, like virtually all eighteen-to-twenty-two-year-olds, were convinced that mortality was something that happened to someone else.

"It's something our moms think about a lot," said Erz, acknowledging the topic had come up at home.

The visit from Tyson Quink, however, was hard for Erz

and the other Firsties to slough off. He doubted that Tyson remembered him, but Erz certainly knew who Tyson and Tera were from when he was a Plebe.

"You have this image of him as a Firstie and one of the bigger guys on our line, and then three years later he doesn't have any legs," Erz said. "It's real and it's out there, and if people aren't buying into it by now, I don't know if you can get more real life than that."

The previous season the Black Knights had a front-row seat to another terrible but different type of tragedy. Their slotback Malcolm Brown fielded a kickoff in the fourth quarter of a game against Rutgers. Eric LeGrand, a defensive tackle for the Scarlet Knights, bore down on Brown. LeGrand was six foot two and 275 pounds. Brown was five foot eleven and barely 200 pounds. LeGrand's helmet slammed into Brown's left shoulder. Both fell to the turf. Only one got up. LeGrand had been paralyzed from the neck down.

Brown and LeGrand, as well as the players from both teams, had been linked ever since. They exchanged letters and phone calls. Over the summer, Coach Ellerson took Malcolm, Erz, Max, Trent, and A-Rod to the hospital where Eric, confined to a motorized wheelchair, was rehabbing, and the group spent several hours with him. There was no media coverage or photo opportunity. The visit was simply a way to offer encouragement.

Malcolm remained haunted by the accident. He could not sleep for days. About a month later, he put pen to paper and wrote LeGrand a letter.

"It was difficult watching you get carted off the field," he wrote. "It really put the game in perspective. It made me realize that despite being on different teams we are all brothers on the field working to accomplish the same goals and playing our hearts out for the game we love. I just want to say, Stay strong, keep your head up and trust in the Lord. Everyone here at West Point is keeping you in our prayers and wishing you a fast recovery."

The visit to LeGrand had hit close to home for Erz and his teammates, just as the visit from the Quinks had the previous Friday. The trick was not letting it hit too close—to compartmentalize it, to push it away.

"It's terrible," Erz said, "and you pray for those guys and hope they recover and get the strength to do that. Football isn't war. It's a game we play for fun."

He paused. War was war. And Tyson Quink had made plain what could happen during it.

"Really, if you dwell on it, you're more likely to get hurt," he said, and then shrugged. "If it's in God's plans, it's in God's plans."

At any rate, Erz still had time to decide on what his second branch choice might be as well as consider whether or not Infantry was worth asking for an ADSO to extend his military commitment to eight years.

His most immediate problem was the one he was going to wrestle with for the remainder of the season. How was he going to lead the Black Knights? The day before, Sunday, Erz and Max and A-Rod had called a players-only meeting after the team's yoga session. Erz was not a rah-rah guy or an ass chewer, and he was doing his best to grow into a motivator without striking any false notes. The previous season Steve Anderson was a captain and was the emotional presence and the voice of the Black Knights. He wasn't the biggest or fastest player on the squad, but he had a nose for the ball and played with a fury that was intimidating even to his teammates. Anderson was everything Erz was not, nor were Max and A-Rod.

In fact, Coach Ellerson marveled at how A-Rod's manner on the football field was so mild that it would not have been out of place in church. Off the field, he conducted himself like a general's son, conscious that his professors and fellow cadets were aware of his father's legacy and were measuring him against it. So Andrew stayed occupied. He was hyperefficient, always had his head in a book or was hunched over his calculator.

Ellerson admired his captains greatly, but he also would have felt better if this young team had a more fearsome force to respond to in the locker room as well as the barracks. When Anderson talked, exploded really, his teammates snapped to. Erz was more cerebral and had excelled the previous season because he could manage and communicate to his teammates the adjustments the coaching staff made to the double-eagle flex throughout the game while Anderson torched their souls and boiled their testosterone. Ellerson understood that the players were asking a lot of Erz this season. They needed him to continue to play with his trademark relentless effort but to be a presence, a wise man, in the locker room as well. His twenty-one tackles against Northern Illinois demonstrated he could do the former; before his teammates now, he was trying to prove he could do the latter.

Erz told them their wake-up call had been delivered by Northern Illinois and that he wanted to make sure they had heard it. His tone was calm but firm as he told his Army teammates that the next three games would set the tone for the remainder of the season. He asked them to smart a little from the beating they took but then get back to work.

"You don't get your ass kicked like that and not be disappointed," he said evenly. "We can tell you younger guys to run to the ball and to pay attention to your assignments, but I think we all got a taste out there of what happens when you don't do what you're supposed to do."

Max and A-Rod reinforced what Erz had said and spoke about what they expected against San Diego State rather than dwelled on what had happened at Northern Illinois. Upon the team's return to campus on Sunday morning, Max had called his brother, Ross, who was working as a graduate assistant for the football team at Eastern New Mexico University. It was four thirty in the morning at West Point, but Max knew that Ross would be awake and breaking down game film of Eastern New Mexico's 43–36 loss in overtime to New Mexico Highlands University. Max wanted to hear his brother's voice as well as get his help. Ross had been a quarterback at Louisiana Tech, completing 438 passes for 5,036 yards and thirty-six touchdowns. He had experience keeping troubled teams together. The first thing big brother did, however, was congratulate Max for throwing the first touchdown pass of his career. It embarrassed Max. He would rather have not played at all in a victory than achieve a career milestone on the losing end of a rout. Ross told Max not to panic and to remind his team of what had worked for them the previous season. He told him to keep it simple as well. That is what the Army cocaptain did.

"Snap and react," Max told his team. "We got to get back on the edge and be accountable."

The Black Knights also needed to remember the motto that Ellerson had brought with him to West Point. They had to stay together as a team. Erz, Max, and A-Rod may have sounded like lawyers rather than locker-room preachers, but each was on the lookout for any outliers or malcontents. They did not expect to find any, not this early in the season with a team this young and inexperienced. They had played on bad teams as well as on good ones in the previous three years, and they knew that backbiting and finger pointing were the surest route to a disastrous season.

"We don't have a top NFL draft pick who can take over the game," Max reminded them. "We got to stay together."

Erz thought the meeting had gone well—or at least he hoped it had. He would know for certain by how the team practiced in the ensuing days. In the meantime, Erz took comfort in what he understood about himself and what he had learned after thirty-nine months at West Point.

The first was that he was not, and never would be, a screaming, kick-the-locker type of leader. "You kick the locker, you break your foot, and then you're done," he said.

This also was not a place for second-guessing. About Eric LeGrand or Tyson Quink or a football game that was played on the previous Saturday.

"West Point doesn't give you much time to dwell on what happened," Erz said. "There is always something more important coming at you."


The game against San Diego State was more than Army's home opener and a contest that the Black Knights needed to win to put their season back on track. It was being played on Saturday, September 10, 2011, the day before the tenth anniversary of the 9/11 terrorist attacks that claimed nearly three thousand lives at the World Trade Center, the Pentagon, and on the hijacked United Airlines Flight 93 that crashed in a field near Shanksville, Pennsylvania. There were tributes and memorials taking place across the country all weekend. The terrorist attacks were to be remembered on game day as well with former New York mayor Rudy Giuliani on hand to salute the firefighters, police officers, and soldiers who had distinguished themselves since.

There are perhaps no words to summon how dramatically that day changed the United States and its citizens. It put the names Osama bin Laden and Al Qaeda into the national lexicon and introduced fierce debate about everything from public safety to civil liberties to torture. It prompted wars in Afghanistan and Iraq that have claimed the lives of more than six thousand service members and had a profound effect on the past, present, and future cadets at the United States Military Academy. Former cadets have accounted for a higher proportion of the dead in Iraq and Afghanistan than in any other recent wars. In Iraq and Afghanistan, about 1.4 percent of the U.S. dead have been former cadets, a ratio three times higher than in Vietnam or Korea, six times higher than in World War II, and thirteen times the proportion of those killed in World War I. The reasons range from a new and savage kind of warfare—suicide bombers and improvised explosive devices—to larger graduating classes that are putting more junior officers into more perilous missions on the battlefield.

Everywhere at West Point there are reminders that America is at war and that Academy graduates are in its crosshairs. On a recent morning at Washington Hall, the din of more than 4,300 cadets preparing to shovel a blizzard of bacon and eggs and cereal and coffee suddenly stilled when an ominous baritone rang from a balcony above the main dining room.

"Please give your attention to the first captain!" boomed the voice on the public address system.

The sudden silence raised goose bumps. It was as if more than 4,000 cadets had vanished in an instant. Birds chirped. Boat engines rumbled to life. The only sounds were coming from outside this usually noisy and cavernous mess hall.

"I regret to inform you of the death of First Lieutenant Timothy J. Steele, class of 2009," said First Captain Charlie Phelps, the highest-ranking cadet. "First Lieutenant Steele died on 23 August 2011 in Kandahar province, Afghanistan, when his unit came in contact with enemy forces using improvised explosive devices. Please join me in observing a moment of silence for this fallen graduate."

Soldiers from every war since the Revolution have been buried in the cemetery behind the Old Cadet Chapel. The cemetery hosted its first military burial in 1782 and was dedicated as a national cemetery in 1817, a half century before Arlington National Cemetery or Gettysburg. Section 36 is its newest and least elegant addition, with the markers for nineteen soldiers killed in Iraq shoehorned next to a parking lot and guarded by a hedge. Nine were lieutenants and eight were captains; there are also a major and a colonel. Fifteen of them had yet to turn thirty. They left seventeen children aged twelve or younger and eleven widows. Among those killed is Emily Perez, the first member of the class of 2005 to die in Iraq, as well as the first female Academy graduate to do so.

The current cadets knew absolutely that they were certain to see combat when they chose West Point, and many look to the September 11 attacks as their seminal moment of inspiration. Members of the Black Knights were no different and had searing memories of that horrifying day. They spoke as if it had occurred yesterday instead of ten years earlier, when they were middle school students or younger.

Malcolm Brown still had to catch his breath when telling the story of his father, Roscoe, a New York City firefighter. Five weeks before the attacks, Roscoe Brown had transferred from Ladder 111 in Bedford-Stuyvesant to Engine Company 28 in Queens. On the morning of the attacks, the men of

Ladder 111 raced to the financial district and were among the first on the scene.

"His old unit responded to the crashes, and not a single one of them came out alive," Malcolm said. "All of his friends died that day. It scared me to think that he could have easily been one of them."

Every day for the next two months, ten-year-old Malcolm watched his father leave their home in Bay Shore, Long Island, for Ground Zero to search for survivors and to recover the bodies of his friends. Roscoe Brown would return as late as 2:00 a.m., stiff, tired, and smelling of smoke. He never complained, however, and headed back to New York City at dawn. His father's dedication over those two months stuck with Malcolm. He understood what a sense of duty could empower.

"It was amazing how much determination he had every day to go back there," Malcolm said of his father. "He was serving the city and he was honoring his old unit. It's what inspired me to come to West Point."

Davyd Brooks, a Firstie wide receiver, remembered hearing his name called over the loudspeaker during fourth-period study hall at North Junior High School in Newburgh, New York. He and his twin sister, Dhavosha, were told to come to the office. He saw his mother, Mary, waiting there in tears. His father, David, was a New York City police officer and among the two hundred first-responding police units.

"My mom tried to explain everything, but it was impossible to understand what had really happened," Brooks said. "When we got home, I immediately turned on the television to see what was going on. We couldn't reach my dad. I got on my knees right there, prayed that he was okay, and left it up to God."

His prayers were answered late that night when his father

pulled into the driveway. It was not until the following year, however, that Davyd heard West Point calling loud and clear. His local paper, the *Times Herald-Record,* had dedicated its 9/11 anniversary section to those families in the area who had lost a loved one on that day.

"It was one of the saddest things I've ever read, but I forced myself to read every last word," said Brooks. "The worst part was looking at the pictures of children with their mothers and fathers that had passed. Some of the kids I went to elementary school with lost parents in the attacks. It struck such a personal chord with me.

"I remember getting very emotional in my room and decided I never wanted someone to have to suffer like that again. What could I do about it? The answer was obvious, and I then decided that I would serve my country in one form or another when I was done with high school."

Ben Jebb was a fifth grader at West Point Elementary School on September 11, 2001, and understood immediately how his life and those of his classmates were about to change. There were no signs of panic on post, but massive security appeared instantly. Gates were closed, civilian traffic was blocked, and snipers took their places on the rooftops. The United States Coast Guard was docked on the Hudson. One truck bomb could have done great harm to a generation of Army officers as well as America's psyche.

Lieutenant General William Lennox was the Academy superintendent on September 11 and was approached almost immediately by a cadet who told him that he wanted to leave West Point and enlist in the Army. He wanted to get into battle as soon as possible. Lennox was proud of the sentiment, but after hearing it what he felt was too often, he took to the poop deck in Washington Hall for dinner on September 13 and counseled the Corps of Cadets to be patient. They were going to be needed, he assured them, as officers. As midnight approached the next night, the cadets stood at attention and heard a ceremonial gunshot over Trophy Point as the bugler played "Taps" in memory of those who had died. Ten years later, Lennox's prediction is still true and woven into West Point's daily life. The faculty goes from classrooms to combat and back, returning with war stories and scars.

"For our generation, it's hard to think of a world where there's not something going on to fight the war on terror," said Jebb. "From fifth grade on, it was all about Afghanistan and Iraq. My friends' parents were deployed at different points. The thought of there not being a conflict overseas is somewhat weird to me actually. Regardless of what is going on when I graduate, I know it's my mission to serve the country that I have believed in since childhood, and it will be my honor to do so."

# 10

"I don't know how good they are, but they are an awfully tough bunch."

—San Diego State coach Rocky Long,
September 10, 2011

Coach Ellerson wandered to the middle of the field during pregame to say hello to Rocky Long, the San Diego State coach. They were close in age—Long was sixty-one—and the two had traveled in the same West Coast coaching circles. They even had intersected in the Canadian Football League in the 1980s, when Long was coaching linebackers for the British Columbia Lions and Ellerson was the defensive coordinator for the Calgary Stampeders. You could not have ordered up a more perfect day for a home opener—sunny, cloudless skies with temperatures in the seventies. Tailgate parties were under way from the banks of the Hudson to Buffalo Soldier Field on the upper campus and all the parking lots in between. Mills Road was closed down and transformed into Black Knights Alley so kids could rock climb or pull helmets over their heads to take on a member of Army's fencing team while their parents grabbed a hot dog and a beer.

Cadets were handing out small flags at the entrances in honor of the "Salute the Heroes" tribute as the first of the 27,000 people filed into Michie Stadium for the noon kickoff.

"It's a beautiful place," Long said as he and Ellerson met near midfield.

"Try to recruit here," Ellerson replied, deadpan.

Both smiled. They had had a similar exchange thirty years ago in Laramie, Wyoming, when Long was the defensive coordinator for the University of Wyoming and Ellerson an assistant for the University of Hawaii. In those days, it was Long who was doing the faux moaning about his tough lot in life in the football wilderness of the Wild West. Now, they chatted as balls boomed over their heads from each team's punters and as their teams moved sideline to sideline, 30-yard line to goal line, during warm-up drills. They shook hands and went to their respective sides of the field.

With twenty minutes before kickoff, Coach Ellerson followed the Black Knights off the field and back to their locker room. He went into the equipment room with some of his staff while his team took seats in front of their lockers. Some of them fired up their iPods and iPhones. Some pulled towels over their heads; others got up and hopped and stretched.

Payam Saadat, Army's co-defensive coordinator, walked between lockers and in a smooth singsong called, "I'm looking for the Army team that sacrifices everything for one another."

"Here, Coach," someone said.

"I'm looking for an Army team that loves each other," Saadat called.

"We're here," someone called.

"I'm looking for the Army team that a sixteen-year-old boy

looks up to," said Saadat, referring to Cody, a young boy with cancer who had spent a day with the Army team earlier in the week as part of the Make-A-Wish Foundation and was attending the game.

"Yeah, Coach, we're here," someone answered, satisfying Saadat and sending him back to the rest of the coaches.

"They don't come into our house on the anniversary of 9/11," cried out Max.

"They can't wait to get back to the beach," said Davyd Brooks.

Joe Bailey, a Firstie and starting offensive guard, was working himself into a lather. He was a squat, 260-pound Georgian who liked what Lieutenant Colonel Vermeesch had told them the previous week. Bailey made it his own.

"They haven't done CTLT, CLDT, or MTA like we have. Nothing. So fuck 'em," he said, his face flashing crimson. "They've been sitting on the couch all summer with their thumbs up their asses playing Xbox games of shit we were in the fucking field doing."

It not only raised the spirits of his teammates, it put ear-to-ear smiles on their faces.

"Let's get ready to roll, O-Train," called out Max.

"Choo-Choo, motherfucker," Bailey answered back, sending the Black Knights into spasms of laughter.

By the time Coach Ellerson appeared in their midst, his players had their helmets on and were bouncing in the middle of the locker room.

"You guys remember how a football game goes?" he asked, launching into a familiar pregame call-and-response.

"How, Coach?" one player after another shouted out.

"This is going to be hard," Ellerson said, feigning surrender.

"No, Coach," his team yelled back.

"Sometime you're going to look up at the scoreboard and think, *This is easy*," he called back.

"No, no, no," came from everywhere.

"What you got to do is get in the moment and play the next play," he said. "What's expected of you?"

He stared at his team.

"What is expected of you! What we demand from each other and you should demand of yourself is that you're the Army team. You get on the edge and you play the next play."

Ellerson raised his arm and his players leaned in to grab it.

"Sixty minutes, one play at a time on the . . ." he called.

"EDGE," they shouted back fiercely.

They filed out in waves, reaching above the doorway to slap General MacArthur's famous slogan painted above it: "There is no substitute for victory."

Outside, the Pipes and Drums of the Corps of Cadets was blowing "The Caissons Go Rolling Along," sending the Black Knights' adrenaline soaring even higher. Opposite the bagpipes was a row of Army officers and uniformed New York City police and firefighters. One of New York City's finest handed an American flag to Jon Crucitti, a Yearling running back. The cop told him it was not just any flag but one that was flown at Ground Zero in the days after the 9/11 terrorist attacks. Crucitti's eyes lit up. He grabbed the flagpole with both hands. He sprinted from the south end zone between a lane of Plebes in their dress grays and stretching to the 50-yard line with his teammates bouncing and jumping behind him.

Once the game started, it quickly grew quiet in Michie Stadium. Ryan Lindley of San Diego State hit a streaking Colin Lockett for a sixty-eight-yard touchdown on the second play of the opening drive. The Black Knights were able to move the ball themselves on their first possession, driving thirty yards

into the Aztecs' end of the field but stopped suddenly when
Larry Dixon was hit hard at the line of scrimmage and fumbled the ball. San Diego State's Marcus Andrews fell on top of
it. Larry came off the field with his head down and was met
immediately by Jared Hassin, the starter at fullback.

"Don't worry about it," said Hassin, slapping Larry on the
shoulder pads. "Just play the next play."

The Black Knights held the Aztecs and forced a punt, but
once again Army could not take care of the ball. On second
down and eight, Trent Steelman faked a handoff to Hassin and
kept the ball, only to be buried by San Diego State linebacker
Rob Andrews. The ball popped out, and the Aztecs' Vaness
Harris was there to recover it on the Army 27-yard line. One
minute later, the swift, shifty Ronnie Hillman darted through
the heart of Army's defense and then bounced outside sixteen
yards untouched and into the end zone. San Diego State was up
14–0, and it was just midway through the first quarter.

Coach Ellerson stood alone down the sidelines listening on
his headset to his assistant coaches, Chris Smeland and John
Mumford, in the press box as they suggested formations and
adjustments in the hopes of slowing down San Diego State. He
practiced what he preached and focused on the next snap, the
next opportunity to make something good happen. Army's
defensive line had been outweighed by an average of seventy
pounds per man against Northern Illinois's front, and against
San Diego State the weight advantage was close to one hundred pounds. The Aztecs were faster as well.

The Black Knights needed not only to score but also to
mount a slow, long drive to keep San Diego State's offense off
the field. With 5:55 remaining in the first quarter, Army found
its groove. John Crucitti carried for four yards, Jared Hassin
for seven, and Raymond Maples for three more. On second

down with six yards to go, Trent kept the ball, ran down the line, and then turned upfield for a twenty-eight-yard gain to the Aztecs' 28-yard line. The triple option was in gear—Raymond Maples was pounding the middle of the line, while Malcolm Brown and Trenton Turrentine were taking pitches and getting outside for five- and six-yard gains. When Trent took the ball into the end zone from the 1-yard line, the full-throated voices of four thousand cadets burst into the Army fight song for the first time in the 2011 season.

*On, brave old Army team!*
*On to the fray.*
*Fight on to victory*
*For that's the fearless Army way.*

On the sideline, Trent crashed into Max in a flying chest bump, and the Black Knights raised their gold helmets to their singing classmates. The drive had lasted eleven plays, covered seventy-one yards, and chewed nearly five minutes off the game clock. It also had injected some electricity into the Corps of Cadets and all of Michie Stadium.

It was about to get a whole lot louder for a reason that had nothing to do with football. Medal of Honor recipient Staff Sergeant Leroy A. Petry was striding onto the field. The plain-talking Army Ranger had won over the Corps of Cadets, and everyone else who had heard his story, during his visit to campus earlier in the week. He was part of the Salute to Heroes program, and the Black Knights took off their helmets and stood at attention. Coach Ellerson and his staff forgot about football for a moment and joined the standing ovation.

Sergeant Petry became just the second living Medal of Honor recipient since Vietnam for his actions in a rare daylight raid in Afghanistan on May 26, 2008. He was the senior non-commissioned officer among seventy Rangers who were trying to secure an enemy building. He was clearing a courtyard with Private Lucas Robinson when they were both wounded by enemy fire. With his legs shot, Petry managed to pull Robinson to safety behind a chicken coop, where they were joined by Sergeant Daniel Higgins. Soon, an enemy grenade landed ten meters from them, wounding Higgins as well. When another grenade landed just two feet from Higgins, Petry picked it up and tried to throw it back at the insurgents. It blew up as he opened his hand, severing it completely and lacing the rest of him with shrapnel.

Although Petry lost his right arm below the elbow, he refused to seek a medical discharge. He remained in the Army and had a deployment to Afghanistan between recovering and receiving the Medal of Honor.

"He is who we want to be," said Brad Kelly, Army's right tackle, to no one in particular.

The Black Knights were a new team in the second quarter and succeeded in keeping the Aztecs' offense off the field. Starting on Army's own 18-yard line, Trent ran the triple option like it was second nature. Over fifteen plays and nearly eight minutes, six different Army ball carriers moved the ball down the field. They even got a break when Trenton Turrentine was able to recover his own fumble on San Diego State's 11-yard line. The next play, Trent took the ball around the corner for a touchdown. When Alex Carlton converted the extra point, Army ended the first half in a 14–14 tie.

The Black Knights moved purposefully in the locker room at halftime. The special teams met in the front of the room with Coach Joe Ross, the offensive linemen in the corner with Coach Gene McKeehan, and the defense with Coach Saadat.

Trent Steelman had hobbled to the training room to get his right ankle and chest retaped. He had gained seventy-four yards running the ball but had taken some punishing hits in the process. He grimaced as an Ace bandage was stretched beneath his armpit. In the hallway, Coach Ellerson was listening to Ian Shields, his offensive coordinator, tell him what was working and what wasn't. Both were exasperated by Army's five fumbles in the first half. Turnovers had hurt them badly at Northern Illinois, and they threatened to do the same against the Aztecs.

"Looks like the Army team showed up today," Ellerson said as he strode into the center of the locker room. "Don't look at that scoreboard. Remember, play the next play."

As they emerged from the locker room, they were stopped in the end zone as an American flag the size of the field was unfurled. Mayor Giuliani was wrapping up his speech, and the field was lined with police, firefighters, and paramedics who had been among the first responders at the World Trade Center a decade earlier. The mayor was no stranger to West Point. He had been coming to games here since the mid-1980s. He spoke about the generation of leaders that had emerged from West Point and how grateful America was for them.

"They have preserved, protected, and defended America," he said. "The burden of carrying on that defense falls disproportionately on the shoulders of the young men and women educated here at West Point."

The Black Knights were ready to get back on the field but were stopped in their tracks once more. Sergeant First Class MaryKay Messenger and the United States Military Academy Band cued up "God Bless America." Their helmets came off once more, and they stood at attention and sang along. The Aztecs were standing alongside the field as well with their helmets off, many of their players gazing wide-eyed at the scene. It was the first time San Diego State had ever played Army, and Coach Long had done his best to prepare them for the spectacle of Michie Stadium, but on an afternoon like this it could be more than a little overwhelming.

The Black Knights were a confident team on their first drive of the second half and had the Corps of Cadets at full throttle as they marched down the field. Malcolm Brown ran around end on back-to-back carries of six and five yards. Larry Dixon burst up the middle for ten yards, and all of sudden Army was on San Diego State's 37-yard line. On the next play, however, the Aztecs pried the ball loose from Jared Hassin, who managed to recover it but for a loss. It was fourth down and two on the Aztecs' 29-yard line, just outside the range of Army's field goal kicker, Alex Carlton. Coach Ellerson decided to go for it on fourth down. Trent Steelman handed the ball to Larry, who slammed straight into San Diego State's Logan Ketchum. Larry had kept his legs moving but was still a foot short of the first down.

With 5:14 remaining in the third quarter, San Diego State found the offense it had been missing since the first quarter, in the form of their 190-pound running back Ronnie Hillman. The sophomore slipped and slid through the grasp of Erz and A-Rod and the rest of the Black Knights on a drive that saw him carry six times for eighty yards and ending with him scampering twenty yards for a touchdown to give San Diego a 20–14 lead. The Black Knights caught a break when the Aztecs' kicker, Abelardo Perez, missed the extra point.

Once more, Army answered, this time quickly. Malcolm Brown got loose in open field for a thirty-one-yard gain. Trent Steelman kept the ball for nine yards, and Jared Hassin rolled up the middle for nine more. When Trent kept the ball and swung seventeen yards and over the right side for a touchdown to tie the score at 20–20, the Corps of Cadets and everyone else at Michie Stadium were on their feet. This time, however, it was Army's Alex Carlton who missed the extra-point attempt.

San Diego State went back on top on its next possession with the help of the Black Knights. Army safety Tyler Dickson closed fast on San Diego State running back Walter Kazee at the end of an eleven-yard run, and the two hit helmet-to-helmet, drawing a fifteen-yard penalty against Dickson and giving the Aztecs a first down inside Army territory. When Erz stuffed Kazee and A-Rod hurried Lindley into a poor throw, Abelardo Perez was sent out to try a forty-two-yard field goal. He hit it, and San Diego State had a 23–20 lead with 9:29 left in the game.

"This is our drive," Trent said as he rallied the offensive unit on the sideline. "We're taking it all the way down. Let's get ready."

Two plays later, however, Trent was back on the sidelines while Army trainer Tim Kelly assessed the damage after Trent took a helmet to the chest at the end of an eight-yard run. Max Jenkins was going to have to take Army to the end zone. He ran the ball himself for a first down and followed it up with a tough four-yard gain where he bounced off two tacklers. Jared Hassin and Malcolm Brown carried inside, outside, and then back inside again to reach San Diego State's side of the field. On first down, Max dropped back to pass and had Jared McFarlin open twenty yards downfield in the right flat. The ball arrived at the same time as an Aztec defender, and McFarlin could not hold on. When Jared Hassin was stuffed at the line of scrimmage on third down, Coach Ellerson had no choice but to go for it on fourth down and three on San Diego State's 46-yard line.

On the sidelines, the Army players were waving their arms, asking the cadets and the crowd for some quiet. Max bent beneath the center and, with a quick count, handed the ball to Raymond Maples, who slashed inside six yards to San Diego State's 40-yard line for a first down.

Trent slapped five with Max as he returned to the field. His friend, his backup, had done his job, and the Black Knights needed just 20 more yards to get to the 20-yard line and into Alex Carlton's field goal range for a tie. And they had plenty of time, more than three minutes, to march downfield for a touchdown and the victory. It looked as if that was what they were going to do when first Raymond Maples ran for 6 yards and then Larry Dixon bulled 4 more yards up the middle. All 27,000 people were on their feet after Trent banged out 6 more yards and had another Army first down on San Diego State's 25-yard line. Trent, however, was slow to get up. When he did, it was clear he was hurting too much to be effective, and he left the game for good. He had rushed twenty-one times for a career-high 157 yards and three touchdowns.

Max was going to have to finish the job. He had plenty of time to author a storybook ending, but he needed a little help. He didn't get it. Malcolm fumbled on the next play—the team's eighth of the game. Army's Frank Allen managed to recover the ball but for a four-yard loss. When Max's pass to Malcolm was broken up, Army faced a third-and-fourteen from San Diego State's 29-yard line. They needed to get at least to the 20-yard line for a field goal attempt to tie or down to the 15-yard line to keep the drive alive. Instead, Raymond Maples jumped offside, earning a five-yard penalty back to the 34-yard line. On the next play, Max was sacked. Suddenly, it was fourth and twenty-five from the 40-yard line. Army had time—1:06—but it needed a first down.

Once more Max dropped back to pass, looking for Jared McFarlin, and once more McFarlin could not bring the ball down. It was San Diego State's ball. The Black Knights had outgained a bigger and better team 446 yards to 292 yards, but the eight fumbles and one key penalty had denied them a victory. When Coach Ellerson crossed the field for the postgame handshake, a relieved Long met him at midfield.

"I don't know how good they are," Coach Long said, "but they are an awfully tough bunch."

It was quiet in Army's locker room. The players were too disappointed and too exhausted to begin peeling off their uniforms. Erz leaned against his locker. Trent had his head in his hands. A-Rod still had on his helmet. Max slowly picked his way through the crowd, offering a handshake and quiet words of comfort.

The players circled around Coach Ellerson, and for the first time all afternoon he removed his ever-present camouflage ball cap. He was spent as well and waited quietly until his team took a knee before him.

"Make no mistake, those guys were every bit the challenge that SMU was," he said, referring to the team they had beaten last year in the bowl game. "You spotted them a bunch of turnovers, but you didn't care. You were the Army today."

He let that thought hang there in the silence.

"You turned off the scoreboard and you fought and you competed and you played," he said, letting his cadence pick up steam. "Guys got hurt and other guys came in and fought and competed and played. We were still trying to win the game on the last play."

Then he stopped.

"Guys, I'm not trying to make you feel good for not winning," he said. "You should hate it. There is no substitute for victory. Nobody in the world knows that better than we do. But you have to know this: if you grow like that, if you be that team and keep the arrow where it is right now, guys, we're going to sing a lot.

"We can't sing right now," he continued. "I don't want you to feel good about coming close. There's ten thousand things we got to do better as coaches and players but keep that arrow up."

He paused.

"Hold on to each other," he said. "That was the Army team. Shit, I'll coach that team any day of the week and twice on Sundays. You fought, you fought, and you fought. I'm proud of you."

Ellerson then stepped through them and out to the hallway where Brian Gunning, the sports information director, and Bob Beretta, an associate athletic director, waited. They were there to escort him upstairs to speak with the radio broadcast team and then on to a postgame press conference. Wordlessly, he took a stat sheet from them and glanced at it as he started up the stairs. Coach Ellerson was alone and out of sight when he stopped at the top of the stairs.

"Damn," he said, loud enough for it to echo down the corridors.

## 11

––––•————————————•––––

> "I was too caught up in being superhuman. I wasn't setting goals for myself. I thought I was trying to be the best but I was one-dimensional. I was just a football player. My goal now is to make things little instead of too big, to understand something today that I didn't yesterday."
>
> —Trent Steelman, September 13, 2011

Trent Steelman was always the first to arrive at the football complex, more often than not riding the school bus up the hill by himself at one thirty or two in the afternoon. It's how cadets got around the sprawling campus, especially the varsity athletes who were too beat or too harried to make the steep climb up the bluff to lacrosse, basketball, hockey, or football practice. It was a gentle stop-and-start ride that was perfect for a ten-minute catnap. The cadets leaned their heads against the windows and shut their eyes to give their brains and bodies a rest. They would lurch awake when the doors groaned open and would put in their hours in the training room and on the practice field, then in the football team's case, catch dinner and a movie. That was Coach Ellerson's euphemism for a meal and viewing of the game film for the next opponent, which this week was Northwestern University, a team that had won its first two games and that many predicted to contend for the Big Ten Conference crown.

Trent was beat up as he usually was. In fact, Tim Kelly, Army's trainer, and his staff were some of the busiest in the nation as they tried to patch together undersized, often exhausted football players for the upcoming Saturday. This was not Alabama or Michigan, where three-hundred-pound linemen scarfed down twelve thousand calories a day of training-table meals, took just twelve hours of classes during the season, and had tutors at their disposal to make sure they showed up for class and did their homework. Trent and Erz were taking twenty-one hours of credits and A-Rod twenty-four. There were no easy As on their schedule, either. All cadets—football players included—were required to take twenty-six core classes and earn bachelor of science degrees. The boast was that each cadet was given a $250,000 education for free. Graduates agree it is worth it but add with a wry yet proud smile that the cost of that education "was shoved up your ass, a nickel at a time."

*U.S. News & World Report* had just announced its "2011 America's Best Colleges Rankings" and ranked West Point the "Top Public Liberal Arts College" for the third consecutive year. Its undergraduate engineering program was named the third best in the nation. In the Best Undergraduate Engineering Programs category, West Point's civil engineering program was ranked second, mechanical engineering was tied for second, and electrical engineering tied for third. West Point also boasted the second-lowest acceptance rate and the highest proportion of classes with under twenty students.

Warren Bennis, the business and management guru whom the *Financial Times* proclaimed the "professor who established leadership as a respectable academic field," said he had learned the most amid West Pointers during his time as an infantry officer in World War II. "I never heard anything at MIT or Harvard that topped the best lectures I heard at [Fort] Benning," he wrote in his memoir.

It was the twenty-four-hour, seven-days-a-week, 365-days-a-year grind that took its toll on all cadets but was exceptionally cruel to its varsity athletes—especially in a sport as punishing as football. Against San Diego State, because of injuries, four more Black Knights had made their debut as starters and three more played in their first collegiate game, bringing the number of Black Knight first-timers to twenty-six. Erz was the only three-year letterman on the team, and he was playing through a shoulder and labrum injury. He was at least able to fully participate in practice. Derek Bisgard, a starting guard, had missed the San Diego State game with a knee injury and would be unable to play against Northwestern. Malcolm Brown and Max Jenkins each had a stress fracture in one of their feet. In fact, Max wore a boot and used crutches when not practicing. Jared Hassin injured his back in preseason camp, and his pain and stiffness came and went. The three of them had barely practiced this season and, as the year wore on, would rarely be able to participate in drills.

Trent Steelman had contusions on his hips and legs and bruises on his biceps and chest. Plain old pain was his constant companion. He had played despite having broken ribs, a chronic bum shoulder, and turf toe. Trent was tough and hard-nosed, always had been. When he was a boy, his parents had first put him into touch football. After a few days, though, the coaches asked them to move Trent up in age group to tackle football. Their son was too talented and too rugged for the boys in his own age group. When Trent was in junior high school, he broke his collarbone in the preseason and was presumed finished for the rest of the year. Instead, he had a plate inserted into his shoulder and was back in the lineup by the third game.

He came by his toughness honestly. The Steelmans were from raw-boned Southern stock. Trent's father, Bob, had lettered in football at Appalachian State University. His mother, Trish, had competed in more than fifty marathons, had undergone a knee replacement in each leg, and was still competing. His sister, Whitney, lettered in soccer at Wofford College. The Steelmans were in the stands for every game, sporting Army jerseys and rooting for the Black Knights. Even though Trent had chosen Army because it was the only Division I college that believed he could help on the field, he did possess military bloodlines in his family history. His grandfather John Steelman served in the United States Army Air Forces during World War II; an uncle, Tom Steelman, served in the Army during the Gulf War; a great-uncle, Peter Roberts, had been an interpreter at the Nuremberg Trials in Germany and was the United States consul to Venezuela during the Nixon administration.

His Army teammates called Trent the "Man of Steel" for good reason. He could sit in the hot tub, wrap himself with ice packs, survive on aspirins and massages, and make it to the field on Saturday on guts and genetics. Adapting to the Academy, however, had not been easy for him. Trent was not a natural follower, a trait that has its place in West Point's leadership formula. Humility, as well as the ability to surrender your own personality and opinions, is important to the military's chain of command. Trent was a member of the National Honor Society as well as the Renaissance Leadership Club coming out of high school, but he had to apply himself academically. If not exactly a nonconformist, he did have a stubborn streak of individuality that was demonstrated immediately by the incident with a confiscated cell phone in the opening weeks of his tenure at the Academy's prep school and his impulse to return home to Kentucky after just two weeks. Trent's teammates liked him and certainly respected him, but his intensity could be intimidating. As an underclassman, he got on guys for missed assignments, and his frustration was sometimes perceived as cockiness.

Trent was a fierce competitor who could lead the Black Knights down a football field, but when it came to his development as an officer he was hardly a natural. He had been made aware of his shortcomings in one of the Academy's most painful ways. In the second semester of his freshman year, he was accused of violating the honor code and was in danger of being "separated" from the Academy, as expulsion is known here.

The honor code reads simply: "A cadet will not lie, cheat, steal, or tolerate those who do." It was not formally adopted as a code and system until the 1920s, but it evolved organically from the basic tenet observed at the Academy since its founding in 1802: an officer's word is his bond. When General Sylvanus Thayer was the superintendent in the 1820s, he expressly forbade cheating in academics. A century later, in 1922, General Douglas MacArthur formed the Cadet Honor Committee to review all honor allegations. After World War II, another superintendent, Major General Maxwell Taylor, drafted the first official honor code publication marking the beginning of the written "Cadet Honor Code." It wasn't until 1970 that the code formally included the phrase "or tolerate those who do."

One of the biggest scandals in the history of the United States Military Academy was the discovery of a cheating ring in 1951 that implicated thirty-seven members of the football team, including Red Blaik's son, Bob, who was projected to be

Army's starting quarterback. It broke Coach Blaik's heart and very nearly ended his career. Nearly six decades later, Trent Steelman, the freshman Army quarterback, was accused of plagiarism. He thought he had made an honest mistake in sourcing; he had cut and pasted a passage that he failed to properly cite. West Point, however, like most colleges, was hypersensitive to the fact that the Internet and e-mail put sophisticated research as well as prefabricated papers and test answers at students' fingertips. In fact, cheating in the form of intentional plagiarism from Internet sources was the leading honor violation at West Point, according to the Simon Center for the Professional Military Ethic. Trent's case was one of thirty-eight brought in the 2009–10 academic year, up from twenty-two the previous year. Of these cases, 37 percent were found to be violations of the honor code, up from 14 percent the previous year. And 64 percent of the cases in which honor violations were found to have been committed occurred in the Academic Department, an increase of 44 percent over the previous year, again according to the Simon Center.

Like most everything at West Point, cadets are responsible for enforcing the honor code. A brigade honor captain oversees an Honor Committee of seventy-six cadets representing all companies. It follows exacting procedures, and the opportunity for development is built into every step of the process.

As soon as Trent was notified that he was suspected of plagiarism, the process went into high gear. Within twelve days, an investigation was under way. Within thirty-eight days, each side's case had to be prepared, reviewed, and heard by nine fellow cadets. As the process hurtled along, Trent became increasingly angry and frustrated. He really did not understand what West Point was about or how it worked or why the hell he was here other than to play football.

"I thought they were out to get me because of my place in the Academy," he said. "Here I was the starting quarterback and a Plebe."

Trent could have "self-admitted," in honor-code parlance, or pled guilty to the Cadet Advisory Board. In the ten years from 1999 to 2009, according to the Simon Center, 121 honor cases were instigated annually, of which 66 were referred to an Honor Investigation Hearing. At that point in the process, a cadet admits to the violation 35 percent of the time.

Trent, however, was among the 65 percent annually who choose to mount a defense and have his day in court. He thought about transferring, but the one thing that Trent Steelman was not was a quitter. He was not going to leave West Point with his honor and reputation in question.

His honor hearing did not go well. Trent was "found," as being deemed guilty is called at West Point. He then waited two harrowing days for the superintendent to render a punishment. Trent was a wreck. His stomach churned and he was humiliated that he had embarrassed himself and the family name. The superintendent at the time was Lieutenant General Buster Hagenbeck, and he had some alternatives to separation available to him. He could show "discretion." Among the ways to do that was to turn Trent back a full class year or turn him back to a December graduate. Another option was to make Trent enter into a six-month honor mentorship with a member of West Point's faculty or staff.

Over the previous ten years, an average of thirty-nine cadets had been "found" each year, and more than half of them—56 percent—were granted "discretion" while 31 percent were separated from the United States Military Academy. The remaining 13 percent were cleared of the charges.

The difference between a second chance or being booted

outright comes down to a variety of circumstances, including the Honor Committee's recommendation and input from the cadet chain of command as well as from a cadet's TAC officers. The superintendent also considers extenuating circumstances: How egregious was the violation? Was the cadet under duress? He factors in the cadet's maturity and his or her resolve to live honorably. The superintendent determines the cadet's potential as an officer and whether he can lead his troops honorably and if fellow officers want to serve alongside him or her. Ultimately, is the cadet worthy of the Academy's and the Army's continued investment in his or her leadership development?

In Trent's case, General Hagenbeck decided that he had earned discretion and placed him in the honor mentorship program, a six-month program with some overarching guidelines but enough freedom for the cadet and mentor to find what worked best. The goal at the end of the six months was that Trent would be confident enough to choose the "harder right" in the tough situations that were going to arise time and again throughout his military career. It tracked along a twelve-step program and required Trent to keep a journal of forty-eight entries and to teach classes to his fellow cadets about what he did and why it was wrong and how it was going to make him better down the road.

The first of its four stages is admission, followed by reflection, rehabilitation, and restoration. Trent was paired with Major Matthew Benigni, a professor in the math department who was not connected to the football team. Major Benigni had the most input about whether Trent's future at West Point, and in the Army, was going to continue and on what path.

Coach Ellerson had no input on whether Trent was going to be returning to school at West Point, nor did anyone else in the athletic department. The number of big-time college football coaches who can go to bed each night without having to worry about one of their players doing something harmful to himself, their athletic program, or their schools can fit around a four-top in a diner. There is Ellerson and his counterparts at the other service academies—Air Force's Troy Calhoun and Navy's Ken Niumatalolo—and perhaps Stanford University's head coach, David Shaw. The trade-off—at West Point at least—was that when a player did not live up to the Academy's honor, academic, military, or physical standards, the matter was beyond the purview of the head coach. In other words, it is how college sports should be governed but rarely is.

Ellerson not only was comfortable with this arrangement, but sometimes, in his wistful moments, he believed that the service academies could be on the vanguard of a magical and virtuous renaissance of college football.

"I think there's something that's shifted out there," he said. "And I've been going into high schools for thirty-five years. We have a generation of young people that do want to be challenged, who do want to do something with their lives, who do want to be a part of something larger than themselves."

He knew that it sounded overly naive or even foolishly high-minded. But Ellerson had hope. He had been at the University of Arizona when the Wildcats competed at the highest levels. He liked and respected and was even friends with some of the most controversial names in college coaching, especially on the West Coast. Guys like Rick Neuheisel at the University of California, Los Angeles, and Dennis Erickson at Arizona State University were coaches he admired, who had won bowl games but had also run afoul of the NCAA as well as their employers. Neuheisel had won the 2001 Rose Bowl at the University of Washington, but his program was later criticized after more than a dozen of his players were arrested for everything from assault to sexual battery. Erickson had won two national championships at the University of Miami in the early 1990s, but the Hurricanes were put on NCAA probation for three years shortly after he left for bigger money and an opportunity to coach the Seattle Seahawks in the National Football League.

Ellerson understood the pressures that his colleagues were under at the University of Oregon and Ohio State and the rest of the "Hollywood" programs, where victories meant more than keeping a rabid fan base happy: it translated into hundreds of millions of dollars in television contracts and sponsorships that paid for the dozens of other sports that could not pay for themselves. He also believed that the vast majority of college coaches are selfless, honorable, and extremely hard working. Ellerson felt that coaches were engaged in an uphill battle against the seductive glamour, the fantasy of fame and fortune that was corrosive to a young man's development.

He knew the shortcuts a coaching staff often took to feed that beast. He knew about the promises made to recruits that somehow had to be fulfilled. Or the supertalented player on the field who had no business in the classroom and needed somehow to be propped up. He understood there were kids whose right-and-wrong lines were not etched in stone—or anywhere else—but had to be watched over and kept in check since he was now the university's "student-athlete" and the coaching staff's responsibility.

"My argument is with the evolving culture and which virtues we choose to put on a pedestal and what behavior we will or won't tolerate regardless of the bottom line," Ellerson said.

But he thought it was a battle that could be won and that the public wanted to win.

"Maybe it's because I'm here now, but I do think people are

looking for a better way," he said. "I do think all those distractions have taken the fun out of college football for those who love the game. I'm coming across more and more kids and coaches out there who want to do things differently. Who want to do it the right way."

Trent Steelman was trying to be one of those people. Sitting here one year after his mentorship, after he had risked his career at the Academy, he felt redirected rather than rehabilitated. His time with Major Benigni was both psychotherapy and a crash course on the purpose of the United States Military Academy and why he was really here.

Trent could say now that he had made a mistake on the paper he turned in. It was his fault and he took responsibility.

"I was in denial," he said.

He understood what had gone wrong.

"I was too caught up in being superhuman," he said. "I wasn't setting goals for myself. I thought I was trying to be the best but I was one-dimensional. I was just a football player. My goal now is to make things little instead of too big, to understand something today that I didn't yesterday."

He came out of the process with goals that sounded simple but had taken his full focus every day since. He wanted to be a good teammate. He wanted to be a good friend. He wanted to learn to listen.

"I had not done a good job of understanding the emotional makeup of the people around me," he said.

Steve Erzinger and Max Jenkins had noticed Trent's efforts in the preseason. Trent was more patient with his teammates. He handed out compliments and told them when they did something well. He was almost gentle.

"Getting the best out of other people," Trent said, "is better than being the best."

Trent wanted to be a good cadet, which meant being fully engaged. He had gone through Beast Barracks but had also undergone knee surgery and was on medical leave for recovery the summer after his sophomore season and did not participate in field training. He did his time at Camp Buckner over the summer. He woke up at five in the morning each day to lift weights and then forgot about football the rest of the day. He was relaxed, mellow even. His work with Major Benigni had prepared him to embrace his Corps responsibilities. Still, he was surprised at how easy it was to disappear into the woods, into his duties, and how much he enjoyed leading a squad of cadets, not just an offense.

"I'm still figuring out how this all works," he said. "But my eyes are open and exploring all my options. There are so many different levels to understand about who you are and where you fit here. I'm not sure where I fit yet, but I'm working on it."

## 12

―――――――

"We learned how much emotion you have to bring to the game, how much resilience you have to bring to the game, what it's like to turn the scoreboard off and play the game you love to play. Now, we have to be better at what we do. We have to be more precise at what we do. If we can do that, if we can bring that same passion, aggressiveness, and resilience to the contest with better execution, with more guys with their eyes and feet right, with more guys coming out of their shoes, we can compete on this stage."

—Coach Rich Ellerson, September 17, 2011

Buses full of tourists hug the bluffs at West Point 365 days a year, as the United States Military Academy is as much a tourist attraction as it is a working garrison and topflight institute of higher education. They come from all over, three million annually, from Europe, Japan, South America, China, all fifty American states. On autumn Saturday afternoons, the tourists wear the colors and jerseys of the college team they support as they make a day of it at the only place in the nation where iconic generals, our country's founders, United States presidents, and Heisman Trophy winners built, fought, walked, studied, and played.

On September 17, 2011, the visitors sported neon purple and were alumni and boosters of Northwestern University in Evanston, Illinois. Most of them got here early enough to secure the best seats on the review stand for the cadet parade on the Plain, which was three hours before game time. In the early days of the Academy, the Plain was the forty acres or so of the flat ground above the Hudson. The Connecticut militia was here first, camping on West Point on January 27, 1778. Over the years, it has been used for everything from mounted cavalry maneuvers to artillery training. Until just after World War I, it also was the summer encampment for the Corps of Cadets, its version of Camp Buckner. And until Michie Stadium was built in 1924, the Black Knights played all their home games on the Plain.

It currently is a much smaller patch of parade ground, a perfectly manicured stage of green where the Corps of Cadets puts on a show like no other in college football. The Northwestern faithful were in high spirits as they enjoyed the cadets' high-sheen presentation and the slaps and whirrs of their rifles. There is nothing as surefire as a military review to make you feel proud to be an American. It was another unseasonably warm and sunny day, making the Hudson's blue waters and the valley's greens and yellows look as if they had popped from a great master's canvas. Elaborate tailgates were in full swing, with white tablecloths stretched over folding tables, piled high with chicken wings, bratwurst, crudités, and chips.

Better still for the mood of Northwestern fans, the Wildcats were huge favorites to crush the Black Knights. They were a Big Ten team, after all, accustomed to holding their own against football Goliaths. Northwestern had won twenty-four games over the three previous seasons and had played six bowl games in the past decade. Only two teams had captured more Big Ten titles than Northwestern's three since 1993, and they were college football royalty: the Ohio State Buckeyes and the Michigan Wolverines. The Wildcats were pulling into Michie Stadium with a 2–0 record and sixteen returning starters.

Inside the Army locker room, however, there was a far different mood. Even in defeat, the Black Knights had felt good about their effort against San Diego State. The film on Northwestern also had boosted their confidence. Some teams are tailor-made to be exploited by Army's triple option and double-eagle flex, and the Wildcats were one of them.

Coach Ellerson said as much to Army's athletic director, Boo Corrigan, at practice the previous Tuesday. He meant it. He believed it. He also knew his emotional biorhythms well enough that by the Tuesday of every week during the season, he was absolutely convinced his Army team was going to win the following Saturday.

By then, he had digested the previous week's film and either exorcised his demons or put aside any feelings of self-satisfaction depending on how the Black Knights played. He met with the beat writers and local television reporters on Tuesday afternoons, where he would briefly put a postmortem on the prior game and then explain how Army was going to win this coming week. It did not matter if the New England Patriots were on the schedule, by Tuesday Coach Ellerson and his staff had seen their film, had a plan, and were ready to impart it to their team.

Offensively, Northwestern was explosive, averaging thirty-three points in each of its two games and controlling the football and scoring with its running game, which ranked fourteenth nationally and was averaging more than 275 yards a game.

The Wildcats were built like a Big Ten team—they were big up front: their two offensive tackles were six foot six and six foot seven and each weighed 310 pounds; their guards were both six foot four and weighed 300 pounds. These were great attributes when Northwestern was lined up against the behemoths of its Big Ten rivals, but the Wildcats were too slow and lumbering for Army's squadron of quick, agile 200-pound linebackers and defensive backs who would be slicing in from all angles at higher velocity. The fact that the quarterback for Northwestern, Kain Colter, was a far better runner than passer was also to the Black Knights' advantage. Army's young secondary was usually its biggest defensive weakness. Now, that same bunch could be employed closer to the line to stop the running game.

On defense, Northwestern was as young as Army, with just three seniors and twice that many freshmen and sophomores on the unit. Like the offense, it was built more for Big Ten power football than service academy speed, precision, and poise. The Wildcats had given up seventeen points to Boston College and twenty-one to Eastern Illinois, neither of which had much of an offense. The Black Knights, on the other hand, were ranked number two in the nation in rushing yards with a 353-yard average with a triple-option offense that the Wildcats had never seen before and traditionally bedeviled the most experienced defensive units.

The true test of whether Coach Ellerson had installed his game plan well and whether Army was about to collect its first victory of the season was about to be decided on the football field. As they waited to take the field, the Black Knights were far more relaxed this afternoon than they had been against San Diego State. Joe Bailey was sitting stoically in front of his locker. A-Rod had his helmet on and was staring into space. Erz was relaxed and smiling and looked as if he was about ready to play eighteen holes of golf rather than go bang pads and helmets with guys who outweighed him by fifty pounds.

Trent was submerged in his own world. He may have been struggling to discover who he was as a cadet at West Point, but right here and right now he knew exactly who he was and what had to be done. A slash of black charcoal was smeared beneath each eye and a towel was draped over his head. Beneath it, he was listening to his pregame music of choice. He bobbed his head and rolled his shoulders like a boxer getting loose before a bout to the beat of the rapper Wiz Khalifa and his album *Rolling Papers*. They may have been cadets and future Army officers, but neither Trent nor anyone else on the team were cultural eunuchs. They listened to what everyone else did. They tapped and swiped their iPhones and iPads using the same games and apps as everyone else. They were listening to music and checking texts and e-mails right up to the moment Coach Ellerson strode to the middle of the room and gathered them together.

"Another week, another tremendous challenge," he told his team. "Northwestern is a Big Ten football team, probably one of the better teams in the Big Ten this year. We, on the other hand, this past week got onto a stage with a quality opponent, and we figured out how to play."

They gathered in a knot around him and nodded in agreement.

"Last week, we learned how much emotion you have to bring to the game, how much resilience you have to bring to the game, what it's like to turn the scoreboard off and play the game you love to play," he said. "Now, we have to be better at what we do. We have to be more precise at what we do. If we can do that, if we can bring that same passion, aggressiveness, and resilience to the contest with better execution, with more guys with their eyes and feet right, with more guys coming out of their shoes, we can compete on this stage."

He paused and let that sink in.

"But it's going to take all of that to have a chance," he told them. "In the absence of those things, we have no chance. Given all those things, we belong in this venue and we can compete in it."

Trent took the coach's message to heart.

"We belong here, fellas," the quarterback said in a low voice, tapping his linemen, his running backs, and wide receivers on the shoulders as they passed before him. "We belong here. Let's own them."

Trent was smiling from ear to ear. If he was worried about fumbling—after all, he'd lost five fumbles so far in this young season—it didn't show. If he was worried about losing, you couldn't tell. When the doors blew open beneath the "There's no substitute for victory" sign, letting a gust of bagpipe music blow through the locker room, Trent stopped and took a long look at his kilted classmates honking their hearts out.

"Man, I love them bagpipes," he said, cracking up anyone close enough to hear him.

Trent Steelman was never lost on Saturday afternoons. He was never uncertain or overwhelmed or in need of making his goals small. Just the opposite, Trent was large and in charge under center of the Army Black Knights. It was the place he had started for twenty-eight games now, the place he felt safest. He was the maestro of Army's triple option. He was the one who decided whether to slam the ball in the gut of his fullbacks, Jared Hassin and Larry Dixon, and let them hammer up the middle, or whether to pull it back out. The defensive end would tell him—if the end ran upfield, Jared or Larry got the ball. If he pinched inside, Trent kept the ball and a whole new range of choices was in play. Turn it up inside. Take it outside. Or pitch it to Malcolm Brown or Raymond Maples or whoever was the trailing halfback.

This is what Trent did best of all, and on the opening drive against Northwestern he showed everyone in Michie Stadium how smart and devastating he and his Black Knights could be. He and the offense trotted out to their own 19-yard line and then spent the next nine minutes completely befuddling the Wildcats. Trent read Northwestern's defensive ends as if they were traffic lights and the light was always on green. He was a wizard with the ball. The white shirts of the Wildcats were chasing phantoms east while Larry was rumbling north and Malcolm and Raymond were picking up big yards west.

Northwestern could barely lay a hand on Trent. He cut inside, and spun and scooted outside, and even completed a pass to Jared McFarlin that totally crossed up the Wildcats. The play that set the Corps of Cadets afire and signaled to the purple-clad Northwestern faithful that this was not going to be a walkover came on fourth down and five yards to go on the Wildcats' 38-yard line. Everyone in Michie Stadium who knew anything about the home team rose to their feet. Of course, Coach Ellerson was going for the first down—it was too far for a field goal and too close to punt. Trent tucked the ball in his left hand and felt his way down the line with his right and seemed to disappear behind his teammates' black shirts before being spit out through a gaggle of white shirts and outstretched arms, stumbling the last few feet to the 32-yard line.

"Mr. Referee. Move those chains," came the voice of Army's public address announcer, Rick Zolzer, cuing the crowd.

"First Down, ARRRRRmy," was its thunderous response.

On the eighteenth and final play of the drive, Trent took the snap, faked a handoff to Larry, and rocketed wide off-tackle seventeen yards for a touchdown. He had carried the ball himself seven times and accounted for forty-nine of Army's eighty-one yards and, as Alex Carlton booted the extra point through to give the Black Knights a 7–0 lead, the Northwestern defensive coaches already had their whiteboards out on the sideline, trying to sketch out how exactly their players hoped to slow down Trent and the Black Knights.

They never really did. Trent converted, rammed, and bulled for Army's eight first downs. He led a ten-play drive that chewed up more than five minutes, but the Black Knights' offense came off the field without points when Alex Carlton missed a field goal from forty-seven yards. Another nine-play drive down to the Wildcats' 29-yard line blew up after Jared Hassin was called for offsides and the Black Knights were penalized five yards. Two plays later, Trent was looking for McFarlin again when the Wildcats' linebacker David Nwabuisi burst through on a blitz for an eleven-yard sack, forcing Army to punt.

The Black Knights' defense, meanwhile, was playing a nearly flawless first half. Erz and A-Rod had their helmets in virtually every pile, and Northwestern time and again was facing third down and long. Army's young secondary, however, did not buckle and came up with timely breakups on long third-down passes. Three times Northwestern had to punt from deep in its own territory. Late in the first half, however, the big bodies of the Wildcats' offensive line found a second wind and opened holes for their running back Mike Trumpy and quarterback Kain Colter. It had taken Northwestern's offense twenty-five minutes to find its legs, but it had: Colter found Jeremy Ebert in the end zone for a fourteen-yard touchdown. Wildcat kicker

Jeff Budzien converted the extra point and the score was 7–7 when both teams headed back to the locker room for halftime.

"Turn off the scoreboard," someone yelled as the Army players took their places with their units.

The coaches got busy on the boards. The managers circled and handed out cups of water and energy bars. The Black Knights had been in this position before, just last week. There was still more football to play, and Army would get the ball first to start the third quarter. The Black Knights didn't waste any time, either. Their second touchdown drive looked an awful lot like their first one. It took ten plays, covered seventy-three yards, ground out more than four minutes of the clock, and ended with Trent in the end zone, this time plowing in from the 1-yard line.

For the next fifteen minutes, the Army defense was impenetrable. It held Northwestern to just ten yards in the third quarter and turned the Wildcats' punter, Brandon Williams, into their most potent weapon. Three times he trotted onto the field, and when he boomed a sixty-five-yarder down to the Army 11-yard line, the Northwestern fans exiled to the seats behind that end zone got to their feet and were grateful they finally had something to cheer about. They were silenced, however, when Malcolm Brown skittered up the sidelines forty yards to the Northwestern 37-yard line. They were in a deep funk as the Army offensive line made way for Trent and his running backs to pound their way down to the Wildcats' 14-yard line. On fourth down and two yards to go at Northwestern's 8-yard line, Coach Ellerson sent Alex Carlton in to attempt a twenty-five-yard field goal and, hopefully, take a 17–7 lead with barely seven minutes left in the game.

Alex missed. Once again no points—this time after a fourteen-play, eighty-one-yard drive in which Army had held the ball for eight minutes and twenty-five seconds. Alex's helmet had barely stopped bouncing from the heave he had given it when the Wildcats' backup quarterback, a freshman named Trevor Siemian, swung a pass out into the flat to wide receiver Jeremy Ebert, who, barely breaking stride, took it sixty-two yards into the end zone. The point after was good, and in a scant fifty-two seconds the score was all tied again at 14–14. On the sidelines, Coach Ellerson did not blink or grimace or collapse into a crouch. He paced—north, south, and back again, working his hands at his wrist, splaying his fingers, listening to the chatter on the headset. Trent circled behind the bench where his offensive line sat and found his way in front of them. He slammed his helmet down on his head.

"We are moving it downfield," he said. "Let's take it right at them."

There was 6:03 remaining in the game, and the Black Knights were starting on their own 25-yard line. Jared Hassin popped through the middle for five yards, and then Malcolm Brown took Trent's pitch and jitterbugged to the right and zipped up the sideline twenty-three yards to the Northwestern 47-yard line. The next play, Raymond Maples rolled seventeen more yards to the Wildcats' 30-yard line and another first down. The Wildcats were slow to get up, white jerseys having made a lane in the wake of Raymond's run. Joe Bailey, Frank Allen, and the rest of the offensive line were bouncing to their feet. Now, it was Scott Williams's time to take advantage of the line's dominance. He scooted through a hole big enough to drive a golf cart through for another seventeen yards. Raymond, then Jared, banged into the middle.

It was third down and six yards to go, and Northwestern coach Pat Fitzgerald wanted a time-out. The ball was on the Wildcats' 9-yard line with a little more than three minutes remaining. The Army offense rushed to the sidelines. Beneath the face masks were bright eyes and half grins. Everyone in Michie Stadium knew who was going to carry the ball for the Black Knights. Trent already had more than one hundred yards and had carried the ball twenty-six times. The question was how were the Wildcats going to stop him?

They weren't. Trent rolled, turned, and stumbled the six yards he needed, and it was now first and goal on the Wildcats' 3-yard line. Trent kept the ball himself again and squirted down to the 1-yard line. No one else was going to touch the ball for Army. Once more, Trent plunged ahead, and as his body crossed the plane of the goal line the cannon went off and the cadets' section turned into a roiling sea of white. Trent pointed his right hand to the sky. He pumped his fist once. Then he pumped it again.

Max Jenkins was on the 10-yard line to meet him. Trent was shuddering. A tear rolled down his face and smudged his eye black, then another one. He slid between his teammates on the sidelines and went and found every member of his offensive line and thanked them.

There were still a little less than three minutes left to play, and the memory of Northwestern's sixty-two-yard touchdown pass lingered on the Army sideline. No one was on the bench when the Wildcats took the field. It didn't take long for Trevor Siemian to hook up with Jeremy Ebert again, this time for eighteen yards, to the Army 43-yard line. Siemian dropped back again, but this time Army linebacker Nate Combs was on top of him in an instant, and the Wildcats lost a yard. Siemian hit wide receiver Rashad Lawrence for seven yards, but on third down and four yards to go the Wildcats' running back Jacob Schmidt ran straight into the arms of A-Rod short of the first down.

It was now fourth down and one yard to go on the Army 33-yard line, and nobody was sitting in the seats at Michie Stadium. Siemian once more went to the air and Ebert, but Justin Trimble got a hand on the ball and the Black Knights held. Trent took the field to run out the clock, fighting back tears as he and his teammates were in "Victory" formation. He took the snap, fell to both knees, and then tossed the ball to the referee. The Black Knights had their first victory of the season, and it had come against one of the best teams they were likely to play all year. They had not merely defeated the Wildcats. Army had dominated them, rolling up 381 yards of offense and holding the ball for forty minutes and nineteen seconds.

As soon as the midfield handshakes with the Wildcats were finished, the Black Knights were in front of the Corps of Cadets for a raucous rendition of "On Brave Old Army Team." Soon after, there was a hush, and the band struck the opening notes of the Academy's alma mater. On the field, the Black Knights cradled their helmets in their left hands and stood at attention. In the stands, the cadets took their hats off and did the same. Then, together, they sang.

*Hail, Alma Mater dear,*
*To us be ever near,*
*Help us thy motto bear*
*Through all the years.*
*Let Duty be well performed,*
*Honor be e'er untarned,*
*Country be ever armed,*
*West Point, by thee.*

Trent, Erz, Max, A-Rod, Larry—every one of them knew the words. They sang loud. They sang proud.

In the locker room afterward, Coach Ellerson was brief.

"You played on the edge," he told them. "We have a chance now. We needed one of these. We've grown. You've got your nose bloodied a couple of times, and we struggled doing some things, but we stayed together and we believed in ourselves."

They had sung and now it was time to dance. The speakers boomed out the bass line to the "Cupid Shuffle," and there was a rush to the middle of the floor where a line of half-dressed Black Knights slid.

"To the left, to the left, to the left," they sang along, "to the right, to the right, to the right."

First, there were six of them, then eight, then twelve, and the line kept growing. Some had better moves. Some had better rhythm. Some had none at all. All of them were having a good time. The party was on, and there wasn't a player in the room not swaying or bobbing to the music. They were cadets. They were tomorrow's warriors. But today they had played a silly game that they all loved. They played it well enough to win. They were kids and had earned the right to act the part.

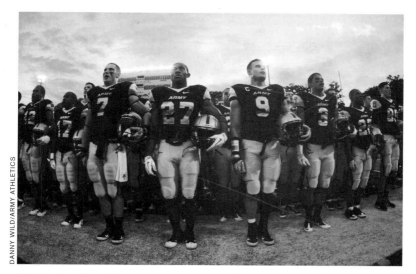

Linebacker Steve Erzinger (No. 9), one of the three captains of the Army football team, leads his teammates in the singing of the Academy's alma mater.

Lieutenant Tyson Quink, a former offensive lineman for the Black Knights, stepped on an improvised explosive device in Afghanistan and lost both his legs below the knee. He met his wife, Lieutenant Tera Quink, at West Point, where she was the first woman manager of the football team, a coveted job once held by General Douglas MacArthur.

Coach Rich Ellerson marching back with a company of Plebes, or freshmen, after Cadet Basic Training.

Coach Ellerson at practice.

Fullback Larry Dixon taking five with his fellow Plebes.

Quarterback Trent Steelman on an UrbanOps mission during summer Cadet Field Training.

Dixon taking a handoff from Steelman in practice.

Steve Erzinger celebrates a big stop during Army's game against Northwestern.

Erzinger leading the team in celebration after the Northwestern victory.

Backup quarterback and captain Max Jenkins was also deputy brigade commander. Here he is leading the Corps of Cadets on the Academy's parade ground.

Jenkins (in headset) and Steelman celebrating a great play.

Linebacker and captain Andrew Rodriguez directing traffic on the field.

Rodriguez and his father, General David Rodriguez, and mother, Ginny, with the Campbell Trophy, which is awarded annually to the nation's outstanding scholar–football player.

Larry Dixon running to daylight in the snow against Fordham.

The Corps of Cadets line up for the march into Yankee Stadium for Army's game against Rutgers.

Max Jenkins, Steve Erzinger, and Andrew Rodriguez meet with Navy's team captains, Alexander Teich and Jabaree Tuani, at the news conference before the 112th meeting between the two service academies.

The Black Knights gathering before kickoff of the Army-Navy game at FedEx Field outside Washington, D.C.

# PART THREE

# COW YEAR

## 13

"It doesn't matter if we're up by fifty points or down by fifty points, the first play of the game or the last play of the game, being an Army football player means we're going to get after you *every single snap*. An Army football player never quits because the men and women who are fighting for our freedom to play this game never quit either."

—Robert Kava, September 27, 2011

The message was from a 1953 graduate and had been left on the answering machine in the Army football office sometime over the weekend. It was a lengthy one. The caller was polite, as might be expected from a West Pointer, but the message had an edge nonetheless. It began and ended with a single question.

"Can you explain to me how Ball State is forty-eight points better than Northwestern?"

Coach Ellerson mercifully never heard it. He did not hear most of the angry phone messages. He did not read the blistering rants on the message boards from graduates. During the season, he did not read the sports pages of any newspapers or listen to talk radio or watch television. He apologized for his self-imposed news blackout to Sal Interdonato, the Army beat reporter for the Hudson Valley's *Times Herald-Record*, after Sal had asked him about the ever-changing landscape of conference realignment in college football. Longtime Big East members Syracuse and Pittsburgh had recently announced that they were joining the Atlantic Coast Conference, and the Big East was looking to replace them, as well as expand with a host of schools, including Navy, Air Force, and Army. Coach Ellerson confessed that he had only the vaguest idea of what Sal was talking about.

"I respect what you do, but I can't follow the news about us or anyone else during the season," he said. "I'm not half as great as I'm said to be when things go right. I'm not half as bad as I'm said to be when things go wrong. I'm human. Things like that get under my skin. I can't afford to be distracted or angry. I got my hands full with my own team, so I just shut everything else out."

Coach Ellerson's hands were, indeed, full, after the Black Knights got absolutely thumped, 48–21, by Ball State, a week after the victory over Northwestern. He was as upset as the caller was and had spent the last seventy-two hours with his staff studying the game film and rummaging through every part of his being in search of how the game had gone so wrong. The Black Knights had taken a step backward, and Ellerson had to find a way to prevent them from falling off the cliff. The facts were stark—Army had a record of 1–3 and was a young, inexperienced, and beaten-up team with way too many tough games ahead of them. Earlier in the afternoon, Ellerson had been cranky with reporters assembled for his weekly press conference because they had pointed out these problems as well as the lofty expectations for this year's team.

The Army faithful expected the Black Knights to return to a bowl game this year and every year hereafter. That is what happens when you take a program left for dead and go 12–13 in your first two seasons and win a bowl game, as Coach Ellerson had. It is the nature of the people who follow all sports, but college football especially strikes an almost tribal need in its fans to be recognized as superior beings. It does not matter whether it's at Alabama or Hawaii or Notre Dame or Cal Poly. The fact is that there are people who live and breathe their teams, and they are the ones who decide whether a coach lives on their sidelines or gets executed and dragged off. There were a whole lot of people who cared deeply about Army football and wanted desperately to see the team win.

No one was calling for Ellerson's job. In fact, the sentiment throughout the Academy was that Army had finally had found the right man for a difficult job. They also had gotten Ellerson at a bargain price. Nick Saban at the University of Alabama and Mack Brown at the University of Texas were at the top of college football's economic food chain with salary and bonus packages north of $5 million a year. Ellerson's $400,000 annual salary, with the opportunity to earn another $350,000 in bonuses, was below the $1.47 million national average of his Division I peers. He wasn't even the highest-paid head coach among the service academies: Ken Niumatalolo at Navy had a base salary of $1.5 million, and Troy Calhoun at Air Force was paid $866,000 and was eligible for another $225,000 in bonuses.

Air Force and Navy not only were willing to spend more money on their football programs, but each was inching closer to the big-time model and were almost certain to join the Big East or some other "super conference." Each maintained high admission standards and were academically rigorous, but Coach Niumatalolo and Coach Calhoun had more control over their players' off-season time and could sell something that Ellerson and Army could not: a less perilous type of military service. The Army meant putting boots on the ground in conflict zones and meeting the enemy face-to-face. As vital and valued as Navy and Air Force personnel are, their service has become increasingly high-tech as America has relied on submarines and unmanned drones. The coaches for Navy and Air Force had the clear advantage when sitting in the living room with a potential recruit, telling his mother and father that not only would their son receive a topflight education and training but it was likely he would never serve on the front lines of a war.

The Black Knights used to be able to win and win consistently. Sometimes forgotten, however, in the yearning to restore Army football to its former glory is the fact that it became a college football powerhouse in the first half of the twentieth century because it had some unfair competitive advantages. Namely, it could bring in ringers. Until 1938, when Franklin Delano Roosevelt ended the practice of "open recruiting," Army's rosters were filled with former stars from other colleges, among them Charles Daly (Harvard, '01), Elmer Oliphant (Purdue, '14), Chris Cagle (Louisiana–Lafayette, '26), and, of course, Earl "Red" Blaik (Miami of Ohio, '18). It was little wonder that from 1890 to 1939 the Black Knights compiled a record of 290–100–29, a winning percentage of .695.

It had been a win-win for all involved. The Academy insisted it had manpower shortages and needed time to train these men to be officers. By attending West Point, these all-star players were able to delay their active-duty commitments.

As good a coach as Earl Blaik was, his Army teams were aided by the onset of World War II and the return to open recruiting. He was hired by the Academy's superintendent General Robert L. Eichelberger in 1940, after Blaik had led Dartmouth to a twenty-two-game victory streak in the 1930s. General Eichelberger believed war was imminent, and he wanted a football team that would be good, and good for America's morale. So Blaik assembled another all-star contingent: Doug Kenna had been a halfback and Barney Poole an end at the University of Mississippi; both became Hall of Famers. Doc Blanchard had played his freshman year at the University of North Carolina and had spent some time in the regular Army before accepting an appointment to West Point and winning his Heisman Trophy. Coach Blaik was as skilled a cherry picker as they come: Army went 68–17–7 for a .777 winning percentage through the 1940s and brought two national titles to the banks of the Hudson.

Army remained among the elite college teams through the 1960s. The National Football League, however, was coming of age, and by the middle of that decade the allure of a potential professional contract looked a lot better than five years in Vietnam.

That was Army's glorious history. It had little to do with Coach Ellerson's gritty, undersized players today. His team had, indeed, gotten walloped by Ball State and now he had to find a way to set things right.

Before the assembled media, however, Ellerson was not going to say what they wanted him to: that Army absolutely had to beat Tulane University at home on Saturday, October 1, to have any chance of salvaging its season.

"All we're trying to do is be one-zero somehow, some way, this week," he said. "The only thing we think about is what happens out there between the white lines. The rest of it is just a distraction, and if that stuff follows us out between the white lines, we'll be in trouble."

He was not going to make a big point that the Black

Knights had to take care of the ball, that eight turnovers in four games were too many.

"If you make it a monster, it becomes a monster," he said.

He was not going to buy into the idea that his team was fragile or not very good or that it was impossible to win consistently at West Point.

"In college football sometimes you're running around in a lightning storm," he said, a bit exasperated. "Our goal is to run around in a lightning storm without waving a three iron over our head."

The Ball State defeat had been costly in many ways. Army's medical ward was getting more crowded, and the on-the-job training of its youngest players was booming. Joe Bailey, the offensive guard, blew his knee out, ending his season as well as his Army football career. It was musical linemen among the offensive front with a previously little-used lineman Robert Kava playing tackle and guard. He was a Firstie with a heart that towered over his talent. There was perhaps not another Black Knight who had bought in as totally to Coach Ellerson and his vision for Army football. Robert was from American Samoa and was the son of a retired United States Marine. He was a squat six feet tall, weighing 250 pounds, and he had essentially willed his way into being a football player. He had appeared in one game in each of his previous two seasons. When you asked him, however, what it meant to be an Army football player, Robert answered from somewhere deep inside and with drill sergeant precision.

"It means being among the toughest group of players our opponents will face on their schedule," he said. "It doesn't matter if we're up by fifty points or down by fifty points, the first play of the game or the last play of the game, being an Army football player means we're going to get after you *every single snap.* An Army football player never quits because the men and women who are fighting for our freedom to play this game never quit either.

"We play for them just as much we play for the men beside us. I have been given the rare privilege to be surrounded by brothers who love this game of football like no one else, who play the game the only way we know how."

The number of Black Knights playing college football for the first time had reached twenty-nine, including twelve freshmen, three of whom were going to start against Tulane. It had been brutal to watch the lessons Ball State quarterback Keith Wenning was teaching to the Black Knights' freshman defensive backs Lamar Johnson-Harris and Hayden Pierce, especially in the second quarter when Ball State gained 234 yards and put up twenty-four points to take a 31–0 halftime lead. The Army secondary were getting run past and thrown over, as Wenning was on his way to a career high of 324 yards passing, including three touchdowns.

"We saw their secondary had a couple weak guys, so we wanted to take advantage of it," Wenning said afterward.

The defeat had taken its toll on Ellerson as well. He was embarrassed. In the second quarter, he called time-out to tell his team he felt kicked in the gut. He told them how disappointed he was that they had not bothered to show up.

"You only get to do this twelve times a year," he said.

Ellerson had wanted to yell at them some more but suddenly lost his steam. He was disappointed and out of words. He stood there in silence, waiting for the referee to signal for his players to return to the field. Ellerson had actually seen this performance coming on the Friday afternoon before the game, when the team was getting ready to leave from Trophy Point. He had gotten a glimpse of Josh Jackson as he boarded the bus to the airport and on the flight to Muncie, Indiana. He looked like a wreck. He asked what was wrong, and Josh told him that he had been up all night studying. The bus had barely left the parking lot, and Ellerson looked back to see Josh and most of the other Black Knights already asleep. He knew it had been a Thayer Week, and they had tests and projects due. He expected the Plebes to not know which way was up. They had so much coming at them and were trying to tread water. The Yearlings, as well, were still recovering from the previous school year and the summer training. Their bodies were recovering and they were still growing physically. Josh, however, was a Cow, and that was usually the year of transformation. He and the rest of his classmates had signed their letters of commitment and presumably had overcome any doubts about service. They had matured physically and understood better how to manage their time. Every day since he had gotten here, Ellerson had pounded into his guys how they needed to have healthy diets and get their rest.

He had leaned on Steve Erzinger and Andrew Rodriguez and Max Jenkins to remind their teammates to take care of themselves and to watch what they were doing at meals. They were his eyes, ears, and example in the barracks.

On the bus, Coach Ellerson asked A-Rod if he had slept much this week. He was brilliant, disciplined, and a straight shooter. Andrew was also fanatic about getting his sleep. He tried to be in bed by nine thirty at night and was mad at himself if he wasn't. A-Rod told his coach the truth. There had been nights during the week when he tossed and turned and could not fall asleep no matter how hard he tried. He had too much whirring through his brain. That might be terrific preparation for an officer who is likely to see through the fog of war, but it was lousy for a football player.

Coach Ellerson's recent predecessors at Army had experienced moments of despair. The most accomplished of them, Bobby Ross, decided he was too old and tired to build Army into a winning program and quit in 2007 after three seasons. He had earned his reputation as a master rebuilder, compiling a record of 94–76–2 over fifteen years at the Citadel, Maryland, and Georgia Tech. None of these was a traditional college power, but Ross's 1990 Georgia Tech team had shared the national championship with Colorado. Ross had taken over two downtrodden teams in the National Football League, the San Diego Chargers and Detroit Lions, and won there as well, going 77–68 in his eight and a half seasons and taking the 1994 Chargers to the Super Bowl.

When Ross took the Army job after three years away from coaching, the Black Knights had lost fifteen straight games, but the old coach was undaunted. He admitted he had been restless at home, but he was confident he could turn Army around.

"You put your entire life into it," he said of coaching. "It's such a strong commitment, not an easy thing to change. It's part of you. You get tired walking the dog. I've got a lot of energy. You never stop being a coach."

In his three seasons, however, Ross's teams had finished 2–9, 4–7, and 3–9. They lost every year to Navy as well. He had been the first one in his office at Kimsey at seven in the morning and the last one out at eleven at night. He also tried to change the culture of Army football, choosing a blueprint better suited for elite programs.

Like Ellerson, Ross looked at the United States Military Academy Prep Schools as a resource and stocked it with fifth-year high school players. By his third and final year, 50 percent of the sixty-five freshmen that he had recruited had gone to the prep school first, or nearly twice the percentage of players that Ross had inherited. He also sent his recruiters out to where the football players were. Before Ross's arrival, 26 percent of the Black Knights were from New England or the Mid-Atlantic states. One third of Ross's recruiting classes, on the other hand, were from Texas, Florida, and California. He wanted athletes and, in search of them, implemented specific size and speed minimums by position for recruits. Ross, especially, wanted to go with size and beef on the line.

Ross was increasingly frustrated, however, with the Academy's administration. He wanted bigger and better players who were thinking football first, rather than cadet life. He wanted their summers eased and their academic loads lessened.

"I'd bring in a 240-pound defensive end and plan to get him up to 260 pounds by his sophomore year," said Ross. "Three months into his freshman year, he would be down to 225. Up and down the weight charts, I'd be wondering what was going on."

Why did these guys have to participate in Beast Barracks? he wondered. Couldn't they skip the daily 5:00 a.m. training runs and hours of marching and drilling in full military gear?

"I learned that we couldn't get that recruit up to 260 pounds until he was a junior," he said. "I learned that at West Point you better not be relying on all freshmen and sophomores to play football. It better be a junior and senior team."

Entering Ross's third season at the United States Military Academy, only one of his twenty-two starters was an underclassman. Eight weeks after a fourth-quarter meltdown against Navy, when Army gave up three scores in less than three and a half minutes to lose 26–14, Ross had had enough.

"I think there's a point in time when you feel like it's your time to retire, and I think I've reached that time," Ross said at a farewell press conference. "I think there is an issue of having a certain degree of energy, which I feel is very important for anyone leading a college football program."

Coach Ellerson, however, was nowhere close to surrendering. Instead, he was back in his War Room and putting a marker to the whiteboard. He was game planning. He was in phase two of building out his vision of an Army football program. He was dreaming a little bit, too. Mack Brown at the University of Texas might be able to scratch a little something on a cocktail napkin and suddenly the permission and the money appeared in his program's bank account. That was not going to happen here, and Ellerson knew that. But the United States Military Academy's command was reviewing the ways, the costs, and the efficiencies of how it did business. If Ellerson could come up with a plan to win nine or ten games a season that was cheaper, more streamlined, and that did not compromise the cadets' military training and academics, he owed it to himself to give it a shot. Isn't that what coaches did? Look for opportunities and attack them?

Ellerson was a clear and concise teacher as well as an enthusiastic salesman when he wanted his team to understand something. He had agreed with Coach Ross that the prep school had been underutilized and currently had thirty-nine would-be Black Knights there, including his son Andrew. He also had benefited from the fact that a prep school building had opened on campus this year. Larry Dixon, and the rest of the prep graduates, had studied and played at Fort Monmouth in New Jersey. Selling a high school senior on a prep school year on the banks of the Hudson amid the majesty of West Point was easier than a remote outpost near the Jersey Shore. The downside? His future Black Knights had no obligation to come to West Point from the prep school and could be picked off by another school, or they could decide that the military life was not for them. Likewise, the Academy was under no obligation to accept them. They had to be admitted all over again, meaning grades and test scores and intangibles were reevaluated.

Coach Ellerson had to look no further than the players crowding Army's training room to understand that his greatest challenge was keeping his guys healthy. Along with Malcolm Brown and Jared Hassin, there were a half dozen others who, once they got hurt, had never gotten better. Scaling back their military duties, however, was not an option. Ellerson was evangelical about the benefits of the grueling marches and summers in the bush far outweighing the physical toll they took.

First, it invested the Corps of Cadets in the team and earned their respect for his players. Before he had arrived, football players were looked at as "shammers" or "Shammerais," the derogatory term for cadets especially adept at getting out of work. When Ellerson arrived, the football team had nearly 200 members, the majority walk-ons who were never going to get close to the playing fields on Saturdays and were rarely active participants in practices. They were on the team because it got them out of company duties or beat the hell out of arduous runs or intramural sports. Ellerson cut the team down to 120 members. He not only wanted his team's practice reps to be meaningful, but he also wanted his players to gain something that he and his staff could never give them and was valuable beyond football.

It was what this War Room and the newest etchings on the board were about. He had made it the cornerstone of Army football. He believed it was the foundation on which all victories in life were built.

"Those trials and tribulations that they've gone through in their first couple years here now add to the equation," Coach

Ellerson said, tapping the board. "We talk about our calluses; we talk about these things we know about ourselves and our teammates that our contemporaries don't know and will never know. Now that's where you start to tap into that. I don't know if you just start when you're a junior, but I know that's when you're no longer paying a physical price."

Coach Ellerson circled some of the words on the board, underlined others, and his voice went up another octave as he found another rush of words.

"I think the younger guys have some of those beliefs and attributes, but they're not going to be as far along from a physical development standpoint maybe as their contemporaries at schools where they are completely focused on just the game, or that's the whole point of their physical exercise. Our guys are tested in other ways. I want them to be."

He wanted them healthy as well, and before him was a way to keep them that way, or at least a start on keeping them healthy. "I'm showing up on Saturday with guys who have weights hanging off them," he said.

He had a plan, one that was going to be tricky to pull off but was in keeping with the spirit of the Academy as well as his own soldiers-before-football philosophy. He wanted his Yearlings to have an opportunity to take some summer school courses in the hope of lightening their load—just a little—for the fall semester. He was not trying to get those cut in half like they do at the University of Florida or Ohio State, but if it was possible to take one class in the summer so his Yearlings could drop down to seventeen hours for the fall, it would be a huge relief.

The way the summer term and training schedules worked now, however, it was nearly impossible. The summers were divided into three blocks of time for cadets, and currently

Block One was for the students who had to make classes up or were in academic trouble. Block Two had classes only for rising Cows and Firsties. Coach Ellerson and Major Bagley were working with the academic department to get additional classes offered in Blocks One and Two for Yearlings as well. Currently, the rising Yearlings—or sophomores—were either cadre members for Beast Barracks or did their Cadet Platoon Leader Training out at Camp Buckner. What Ellerson was asking for was that training be delayed until the following summer when cadets were out at Buckner anyway as part of Cadet Leader Development Training. It was an option offered to all cadets who were injured or physically unable to participate as rising Yearlings. Trent Steelman, for example, had done this after his freshman year and was unable to go to Buckner as a rising Yearling. So he did his training while a cadre leader the next summer.

Ellerson liked his chances—everyone from the commandant to the dean and the registrar were working together to make the kind of meaningful changes that would not merely help the football program but would help develop better cadets. The coach had been impressed daily by the leadership team in place at the Academy and how much thought and effort was put into a myriad of decisions.

Coach Ellerson also wanted to switch practices to the early morning—6:30 a.m. He had adopted that schedule at Cal Poly and discovered that he had a more focused football team in the dawn hours. He did not need to have them for long or to have them hit hard. In fact, the amount of contact this season had started at minimal and was rapidly being reduced to next to nothing out of necessity. Having practice in the mornings also accomplished two other things: it would make his players go to bed at a reasonable hour and allow him and his staff to monitor what the players ate for breakfast, which he believed was the most important meal of the day. Rest and recovery was one of Ellerson's mantras, and he felt that he had zero control over either of them.

"Watch them in the morning," he said. "They shove Cap'n Crunch in their pockets. None of them eat right."

To maximize his players' time, Coach Ellerson was willing to practice on Daly or Clinton Field across from the parade grounds and near the barracks. He was even willing to abandon the football offices in the multimillion-dollar state-of-the-art football center for some space in Building 629. It would be like trading a suite at the Bellagio for a room at the Red Roof Inn, but if it helped Ellerson narrow the gap between his program and Air Force's or Navy's, he was willing to give it a try. He wasn't mad at anyone nor believed he was dealt an unfair hand. He was a football coach, an exasperated one. But he wasn't going to tell his team that.

"I thought I was coaching my ass off," Coach Ellerson said with a shrug and rueful smile. "Now we're back at square one. You can say the right things to everyone but yourself."

# 14

"Some young men and women are just meant to be here, I'm not talking about the overachieving cadets, either. I'm talking about the ones that get here and everything is just right. They may not have known it before they got here, but something goes off, and they know this is the place for them."

—Major Chad Bagley, October 4, 2011

Larry Dixon was looking for someone to hug. He had just scored the first touchdown of his collegiate career, a two-yard burst straight up the guts of the Tulane defense to tie the score. He crashed into offensive tackle Mike McDermott's chest and then banged helmets with guard Matt Villanti. He threw his arm around Raymond Maples and accepted a handshake from Trent Steelman. Larry was beaming. He had put the Black Knights on the scoreboard for the first time this afternoon. He would go on to average five yards a carry, pick up a big third down in one scoring drive, and catch a twenty-five-yard pass to set up another touchdown.

Larry was one of the stars in Army's 45–6 victory over the

Green Wave. He finally felt that he had contributed to his team and that he belonged on the field against Division I opponents.

In the previous three weeks, Larry had felt the game moving way faster than he was. Holes opened in an instant and then closed before he got there. Every time he got hit, it seemed harder than the hit he took the previous time. Larry had expected that there would be a learning curve; that had certainly been the case at the Academy prep school, where the athletes on the junior varsity teams from places like Fairleigh Dickinson and Navy Prep were bigger and faster than any he had faced in high school. Larry had not figured, however, that it was going to be as steep as it proved against Northern Illinois, San Diego State, and Northwestern. He felt as if he were a boy playing against men. Against Tulane, though, all that changed and everything snapped into place like the Legos he had played with as a child.

Larry had demonstrated the power and explosiveness that Coach Ellerson had touted the previous spring when Larry was still in prep school. Larry was a handful on the field, pure and simple, and was among the reasons Army had put in a wishbone formation this season to complement its triple option. Ellerson finally had a stable of big, punishing backs—Jared Hassin, Raymond Maples, Terry Baggett, and Hayden Tippett in addition to Larry—who had the vision to see holes open and the bodies to hurt the defenders who tried to plug them. The triple option relied on the backs cutting through and running away from the defense; the wishbone was about giving the backs a five-yard head start and then blasting into the defense like a missile. There was more potential for violence. There was more potential for hurt, which kept defenses on their heels.

Against Tulane, the wishbone had helped eleven different Army running backs roll to 353 rushing yards and a six-touchdown outburst. It had pulled the Black Knights' record to a respectable 2–3 and had taken their postseason hopes for another bowl game off life support. Even better, it had made for a more festive postgame tailgate. It eliminated the "what went wrong" questions and armchair analysis that accompanied the hot dogs and brats and potato salad after losses. The postgame tailgate was as good as it got in terms of a social outing for cadets, especially the Plebes like Larry. They rarely got off-post, so wandering around the plateaus of parking lots and the grass oasis near the Lusk Reservoir was something all cadets enjoyed. The parents of various teammates were anchored in "A" Lot, right above Michie Stadium, and for hours after the game groups of players shuttled among the various buffets.

Larry smiled as he accepted their congratulations and piled his plate higher with food.

The parents of the Cows and Firsties often were able to take their sons out to dinner, usually just outside the Academy's gates along Main Street in Highland Falls. There were a half dozen or so taverns and saloons like Schade's and the Park, where sandwiches, steaks, and heaping plates of pasta brought in the postgame crowd. Farther down the road at Hacienda, the crowd was younger and included Firsties out to blow off some steam with cheap margaritas. Then there was the Thayer Hotel, which was West Point's on-post Ritz-Carlton in the sense that it was where alumni and overnighters congregated for fine dining at MacArthur's Restaurant or cocktails at the adjacent General Patton's Tavern. There was even the semi-hip Zulu Time Lounge on the rooftop overlooking the Hudson.

The rules for cadet drinking were straightforward enough— you could indulge if you were twenty-one years old, as long as you were not in uniform and did not do so in excess. The Black Knights were mostly a dry bunch during the fall semester, with little time and less inclination to ply their broken-down bodies with beer or stay out late at night. Come spring, however, with New York City a short train ride away and the beaches of the Bahamas and Cancún beckoning, it was another story, especially for the older guys like Erz, whose mentors at West Point had taught him that the weekend passes and leave for Christmas, spring, and summer were precious. It turned cadets into exotic travelers who thought nothing of hopping a cheap flight to Iceland or Europe or the Caribbean if there was a bargain ticket available.

In the locker room, Larry listened to his older teammates as they talked of excursions to Montreal and Aspen and Paris and London. He smiled and laughed but didn't contribute to the conversation. He followed the chain of command up at Kimsey as well, partly because he felt that he had no standing as a Plebe and backup, and partly because it was just easier. The football team was a brotherhood within a brotherhood, and democracy reigned in the football center far more than it did any place else on campus. Still, Larry figured if he didn't say much, then he wouldn't say the wrong thing, and if he watched and listened he would get a little better each day.

For Larry, practice was an escape, a perfect one from the total immersion that West Point demanded. For a couple of hours at least, his noisy brain got quiet, and anxiety about problem sets and rules and regulations evaporated. He hid behind his helmet, bit into his mouth guard, and gave his head over to his gut. He was naturally on high alert on the football field, his instinct launching him into action, leading him into holes, pulling his shoulder low into a tackler. Larry didn't have to puzzle and think on the field as he did the rest of the day.

Being a Division I fullback was a picnic compared to being a West Point Plebe.

The Black Knights were in high spirits after the victory over Tulane. They had played well, washing the doubt that had lingered after being destroyed by Ball State. Larry knew he had been a major part of that victory. The Black Knights needed four more wins to be eligible for a bowl game, and the vibe in the locker room was that this goal was attainable. They could move closer to it on Saturday, October 8, against Miami in Oxford, Ohio. Larry was confident he could help his team do that as well.

All Larry wanted to do in the meantime was lose himself in practice and count the days to Thanksgiving when he could go home and see his mom and his older sisters, Karisha and Shakira. They had come to West Point a month earlier for the San Diego State game, and it had been one of the proudest moments in both mother's and son's lives.

Discipline and determination had helped Laura Ashley to the second-highest level of chief petty officer in the Navy, and she had imparted those virtues to her children. Shakira had graduated from the Art Institute of Seattle and, with her husband, Matt Jarin, was raising their eight-month-old son, Liam. Karisha was married to Staff Sergeant James Stanley and they, too, were living in the Seattle area with their children, Kiyanna, twelve years old, and six-year-old Marcus. Sergeant Stanley was in a recruiting office after serving his third combat tour, his second in Afghanistan.

Larry's mom had demanded accountability from all of her children when Larry was a kid. She knew exactly where he was, who he was with, and when he was going to be home. There was no roaming the streets or hanging out. She knew

Larry's friends and their parents. She did not allow idle time in her home. Larry's outlet was sports. For his sisters, it was part-time jobs and art classes. Larry was in junior high school when his parents divorced, for which he blamed his mother and rebelled against her authority. He took out his anger with hostile exchanges, flagrant disobedience, and "a lot of weekends that I spent at home in my room as punishment," Larry recalled.

But none of that had mattered when his mom came to West Point. She and Larry walked the campus, breathed in its history, and, when Larry took the field against San Diego State, shared a warm heart and a few tears.

"It was really emotional," said Larry. "She got to see how all my dreams had come true. And she gave me those dreams and believed in me and gave me what I needed to climb that mountain."

Now, a month later, Larry was homesick and wanted to hug his mom. He needed some relief from the grind. He may have been one of the stars of the Tulane game, but among his fellow cadets in D Company he was just another lowly Plebe learning how to be a follower. He stayed close to the walls of the building as he walked with his hands cupped at his side and greeted everyone who crossed his path by name. Those were the rules, and only in the classrooms during the school day did they not apply.

"Go Ducks," he called out as three Cows from his company passed. It was the day's mandatory greeting for all members of D Company.

On the Wednesday morning following the Tulane game, he had been up since 6:00 a.m., and a half hour later he had his back pressed against the second-floor wall of Grant Barracks.

The Plebes were there to call out "minutes" in intervals until the 6:50 a.m. breakfast formation.

"Ten minutes until formation," he called at 6:40 a.m, standing at full attention. His voice ricocheted along the tiles and granite in the darkness. Then, Larry and his classmates returned to parade-rest position for another five minutes.

On Wednesdays, a hair inspection was part of the regular formation and often added another ten minutes to the process. It was merely cool this morning, but Larry was bracing for the dark winter days he had heard about, when the snow and the rain and the wind whipping through the valley could turn watery rivulets on your hat into icicles. Larry kept his hair as short as a putting green. His shoes and belt were shined to a gloss high enough to twinkle in the right light. There were other cadets, however, who tried to push the hair standards to the limits—three inches on top and one inch on the side, no strands touching your ears, and tapered on the neck. It was hard to pull off, though, and often resulted in demerits for the vain Plebes, which then were rolled into "hours" and could chew up your weekends with either marching or sergeant's hours, extra duties such as cleaning the bathrooms and common areas.

The inspection was concluded and the march to Washington Hall was on. The assault of more than four thousand cadets on the Cadet Mess is in itself a demonstration of poise, precision, and poetry. They marched in, in waves, and waited behind the chairs at tables for ten until the daily announcements from the poop deck above were completed and they were told to be seated. The Mess Hall's baroque stained glass illuminated battle scenes from American history and bathed the cavernous room in timeless sepia. The mural in the southwest wing soaks up 2,450 square feet and depicts the history of the weapons of warfare used in the twenty most decisive battles in history. But none of the cadets noticed. They had twenty-five minutes to make the food on the table disappear and get to their first class of the day at 7:30 sharp.

Larry was the day's cold beverage corporal.

"Sir, the beverage for this meal is orange juice," he said to his tablemates, members of the football team and mostly upperclassmen. "Would anyone care for a glass of ice, sir?"

Once the drinks were prepared and the coffee, fruit, and yogurt fetched, Larry addressed the table commandant once more.

"Sir, the new cadets at this table have performed their duties and are now prepared to eat," he said.

Then the knowledge questions came fast and furiously at the new cadets who were seated at tables throughout the Cadet Mess.

"How many gallons in Lusk Reservoir?"

"Seventy-eight million gallons when the water is flowing over the spillway, sir."

"What is the significance of Foundation Eagle and where is it located?"

"It is the eagle in front of Washington Hall. Tradition states that if one looks at it during the academic year he or she will not be found deficient in academics."

The purpose of the incessant trivia, the cupped hands, and the rote greetings and formalities was to break Plebes down. Before Larry or any of his classmates could lead, they first must learn to follow. This seemingly useless information may, indeed, be the minutiae of leadership, but by accumulating it and flawlessly reciting it, Larry and his classmates were taking the first steps on the road to a daily self-assessment: "Am I doing enough to prepare myself?"

By the time cadets left West Point as second lieutenants, the hope and design was that they would become so obsessed with that question that he or she had the will and the tools to succeed in any life-or-death scenarios.

Major Bagley had as good a thermometer as anyone when it came to reading a cadet's temperature and understanding where on the journey from new cadet to second lieutenant he or she might be. He had taken the same path himself and then guided thousands of others as a TAC. For the past six years in football operations, Major Bags had had a front-row seat to cadet development, which is even more complicated for the young men who had signed on to play football at West Point. He had watched the lights go on—ever so dimly—for some as late as December of their Firstie year, when they learned on Branch Night whether they were headed to a military career in the Infantry or Aviation or Armor. In Larry, however, he saw that rare cadet who knew where he was, what he was doing here, and why—even in the early days of Beast Barracks.

"Some young men and women are just meant to be here," said Major Bagley. "I'm not talking about the overachieving cadets, either. I'm talking about the ones that get here and everything is just right. They may not have known it before they got here, but something goes off, and they know this is the place for them."

Larry was one of them. He took to the rules and idiosyncrasies of the military as if he had been a soldier in a past life. He absorbed everything from Plebe knowledge to grenade manuals. He walked and spoke with gravity. He pulled for his fellow Plebes to succeed and was generous with his time whether it was helping them study or getting down and doing sit-ups and push-ups with those struggling to pass the physical test. Larry truly believed that stacking Ws mattered—on the football field, on the battlefield, and in life. He was a natural perhaps because he grew up as the son of a chief petty officer who taught him to find the joy in being accountable.

Larry did not exactly relish the Saturday Morning Inspections, or SAMIs, that were conducted twice a semester. But he appreciated the preparation they required—the ten hours of cleaning and the focus needed to master detail. West Point left no room for interpretation on what barracks rooms ought to look like and what was expected from the cadets. The SAMI guidelines ran seventeen pages with photos and were exacting in their expectations.

Larry's bookshelf matched the photos perfectly, usually all the time. His books were displayed vertically, pushed to the rear of the bookshelf, arranged in height descending order from left to right, just as required. There was precision in his wardrobe, too: his white hat, gray hat, and parade hat were lined up from left to right as mandated. His six uniforms hung on wood hangers and were evenly spaced and canted to the right. Larry was competitive, of course, but he was as fired up for his roommate, Casey Childress, who had recently been named "Soldier of the Quarter" for the whole brigade.

"He was the number one Plebe in military standards—that's pretty cool, huh?" Larry said, his eyes alight.

In fact, it was hard to reconcile Larry's childlike exuberance with the serious adult life he was leading. His brother-in-law Matt Karin had turned him on to comic books, and together they had built a collection into the thousands, with Larry favoring the Batman and Outsiders series. He had quickly figured out the tricks cadets had passed down to one another to make Plebe life easier and recounted them with glee. His bed was bungeed together to keep its linens and appearance inspection ready, if not truly hospital corners standard. It meant that he slept on top of the bed with his "green girl," the thermal blanket that was probably the most valued and beloved piece of "equipment" in all of West Point.

"The goal is to have to make your bed like twelve times, in your whole career," he said, delighted that he might be getting one over on military life.

Larry was an eager participant in his duties, cleaning up the bathroom and picking up trash in the hallways. He had not received a single demerit or earned any "hours" or time marching for bad behavior or failure to perform duties. He was a rock star at the "Knowledge Parties" that broke out as well, usually as he delivered the laundry to members of his company as part of his Plebe duties.

All in all, it was pretty tame stuff that passed for hazing these days at the United States Military Academy. Over the years, there had been all kinds of acts of cruelty and physical punishment done to Plebes in the name of building character and toughness. The issue was first addressed by West Point's administration in the years after the Civil War, but despite the attention of one superintendent after another, the incidents of physical intimidation and humiliation continued. General Douglas MacArthur not only testified before Congress, he later wrote in his memoirs that hazing was a staple of West Point culture and practiced "with methods that were violent and uncontrolled." Until 1998, the notion remained that Plebes were at West Point to be tortured and that it was the upperclassmen's duty to see the torture carried out.

In fact, it was sport—the ultimate score was forcing Plebes to quit. They were good at it, too. The attrition rate for West Point Plebes approached 40 percent in the 1990s. West Point in those days was a frightening place where Plebes could be tormented with "shower detail," when they would wear ponchos while being harassed and made to answer knowledge questions until they dripped sweat and became weak enough to pass out. Plebes could be dangled by their armpits on the closet doors, otherwise known as "hanging out." They also lived in fear of being "sharked," a practice in which three upperclass cadets surrounded a Plebe, one in front and one on either side, then intimidated the Plebe by screaming insults and demanding knowledge at a rapid clip. The only safe place on-post for a new Plebe was in his own room.

It was Brigadier General John Abizaid who finally put teeth in the no-hazing policy when he became commandant of cadets in 1997. The following year, he eliminated the yelling and physical punishments and threatened to separate cadets who were caught violating the prohibition on hazing. In the years since, the attrition rate for Plebes has been reduced to 20 percent.

Do not tell Larry Dixon, however, that this is a kinder, gentler era. One evening, like most, he left the Kimsey Athletic Center at 6:30 for his barracks, where he barely had time to pick up his backpack. Then it was off to the library for three hours, until 9:45, when he had to return for trash duty. He would be up until 1:00 a.m. studying for math and chemistry tests and then back on the wall for minutes by 6:30 a.m.

"The worst thing about being a Plebe is not having your voice heard," he said. "Nobody wants to hear you. They only want to see you when they want to see you. You are on other people's schedules. The hardest thing about it is being told what to do, how to do it, and when to do it every single day."

## 15

"We're better than that. We've got to be."

—Steve Erzinger, October 8, 2011

The cannon fired a blank charge across the Academy grounds, the report echoing up the hill to the stadium. It was 5:00 p.m. and time for the American flag to be lowered on the Plain. It's a moment when time stands still at West Point, at the nightly rite of retreat. The cars along the roadways stopped. The cadets and officers on foot turned and saluted. It was Thursday, the one night all cadets were required to eat dinner together in the mess hall.

It meant a shorter practice for the Black Knights and a madder dash to the buses to get down the hill by 6:00 p.m. Trent Steelman and Max Jenkins headed for Washington Hall together. The two were comfortable around each other but were still very different.

Max was the more approachable of the two and got stopped often by teammates and fellow cadets as he made his way across campus. He may have been Trent's understudy up at Kimsey, but everywhere else Max was the man in charge. As deputy brigade commander, Max was the central hub for virtually all spokes of cadet life, from who got what kind of weekend passes to the organizing of receptions for visiting four-star generals and members of Congress. He had an office adjacent to his room in Eisenhower Barracks, and it bustled from morning to deep in the night with members of the brigade staff and his teammates. Max was rarely idle or alone, but he directed his office traffic and shuffled a full deck of tasks like a Las Vegas card dealer—briskly with a warm smile and some reassuring chitchat.

Trent was a quieter presence, moving almost stealthily and in Max's shadow when away from the football field. He did not wear the role of star quarterback easily and preferred to disappear into the library or the quiet of his barracks room. Trent's family was tight, and there had been a large contingent of Steelmans at every one of his games. On the road, prior to games, he gravitated to them at the team hotel. At home, he joined them for the postgame tailgate as well as dinner out in the Hudson Valley.

Trent and Max had both been pleased with the week of practices and were confident that the Army offense was prepared to turn in a big performance against Miami University. Max had reinforced this belief to his teammates on offense, reminding them that, despite their record, there was a lot to like in the Black Knights' attack. The Army offense had rushed for at least 300 yards and three touchdowns in each of its first five games. In fact, the Black Knights were the nation's second-ranked rushing offense, averaging 368 yards a game with at least one player rushing for 100 yards in each of its last four games. Max was confident that the Black Knights could move the ball on the Redhawks, get the victory, and bring Army to the .500 mark for the season. It would give the team the boost it needed heading into the second half of the season and its push toward a bowl game.

Trent knew it wouldn't be easy. The Redhawks were better than their 0–4 record; they were the defending Mid-American Conference champions, after all. They had played well against the University of Missouri of the Big 12 and the University of Minnesota of the Big Ten, only to lose by narrow margins. They also had a highly regarded first-year coach in Don Treadwell, who had previously been the offensive coordinator at Michigan State University, where he had installed an explosive offense. Coach Treadwell had also been a four-year starter as wide receiver at Miami and had captained the team his senior year in 1981. The Miami quarterback, Zac Dysert, a junior, had thrown for only two touchdown passes in the Redhawks' first four games, but he was better than that and becoming more comfortable in Treadwell's passing offense. Dysert was talented. He had been ranked second in the state of Ohio's prep all-time passing yardage list, and he had been the starter for most of his career at Miami.

The truth was that Dysert also was not facing an Army secondary as athletic and experienced as those he had seen at Missouri and Minnesota. The Redhawks needed a victory as badly as the Black Knights. They were playing at home and would be plenty dangerous.

Trent knew something else as well. "We—I—got to take care of the ball," he said.

Against Tulane, the Army defense had played its most complete game of the season, forcing two interceptions and recovering two fumbles. It snapped a three-game string of not recording a takeaway and allowed Trent and the offense to mount long, pressure-free drives.

"We got to take this game from Miami," said Trent, "not give it away like we have been doing."

There was a reason the charming campus in Oxford, Ohio, had been dubbed the "Cradle of Coaches." Miami graduates had earned nineteen National Coach of the Year awards and were among the most legendary names in college football history—Woody Hayes of Ohio State, Bo Schembechler of the University of Michigan, and Ara Parseghian of Notre Dame are all in the College Football Hall of Fame. Two other Miami graduates had a profound impact on the professional game— Paul Brown of the Cleveland Browns and Cincinnati Bengals and Weeb Ewbank of the Baltimore Colts and New York Jets, both of whom are members of the Pro Football Hall of Fame in Canton, Ohio. Two former Army head coaches had also matriculated at Miami and had won national titles as college coaches—Paul Dietzel and Red Blaik. In fact, before the game, a statue of Coach Blaik had been unveiled in the Cradle of Coaches Plaza, which loomed beyond the south end zone of Miami's Yager Stadium. This was a place where the ghosts of coaching greats were celebrated.

Army was no stranger to the Mid-American Conference, having been playing its member teams with increasing frequency over the past six years following a failed experiment as a member of Conference USA. The Black Knights had an all-time record of 21–15 against Mid-American Conference teams, though they were 0–2 for the season after being beaten by Northern Illinois and Ball State.

In 1998, after being an independent for 108 years and in an attempt to move into the mainstream of college football,

Army became a football-only member of Conference USA. It was a move that was supposed to increase Army's national exposure with more television coverage and the opportunity to compete for an automatic berth in the Liberty Bowl in Memphis, Tennessee, which was reserved for the conference champion. Instead, Army found it was outclassed by an array of schools that not only did not share its academic mission but also were hardly the household names that dominated the national college football conversation. Over seven seasons, the Black Knights were 13–67 against Conference USA members such as the University of Cincinnati, the University of South Florida, and the University of Alabama at Birmingham. Worse, by joining the conference, Army had severely limited its scheduling options. With eight conference games and the interservice games against archrivals Navy and Air Force, the Black Knights had only one or two opportunities to schedule a national opponent like Notre Dame or a regional one like Rutgers.

So Army became a football independent again and set out to make itself relevant by putting together a schedule that mixed marquee opponents with some that Army believed it could not only compete with but defeat. Northwestern represented the former and the Mid-American teams the latter. Teams in the MAC, as the conference is known, shared a similar football DNA with Army. Its players had been turned away by the big Division I schools, often because they were undersized or had more heart than talent. Like the Black Knights, the MAC teams played hard and loved the game.

Trent had been especially determined that a prepared Army team was going to show up, not the sluggish and sloppy team they had been in their two previous road games. In the locker room and on the field for pregame warm-ups, Trent came out of his shell and stalked from running backs to receivers, offensive linemen to defensive backs, slapping pads and leaning in with loud encouragement. Trent was fired up, on his toes, eager to compete, and he wanted his team to match his intensity. He was starting his thirty-first consecutive game, to surpass Leamon Hall and become the quarterback with the most consecutive starts in Army's history. He looked every bit the part of a record breaker from the very first drive. His sleight of hand on the ball fakes triggered a seventy-yard scoring drive that drained five minutes from the clock.

Trent was even more impressive with his arm. With four minutes left in the first half, he dropped back and launched a forty-five-yard pass that was so pinpoint in its accuracy that it could have been launched from a drone. Malcolm Brown ran under it for a touchdown as well as Army's longest passing play of the season, and the Black Knights went into the locker room with a 21–14 halftime lead.

The Black Knights were not as confident a group in the locker room as they should have been with a seven-point lead after a pretty decent first-half performance. Steve Erzinger sensed the foreboding in the air. Because of injuries, the Black Knights defense was getting younger rather than more seasoned. There were three sophomores and two freshmen in the starting lineup against Miami, and there were too many times in the first half that they were out of position. In the first quarter, Miami had scored twice on passes, and Zac Dysert was starting to look more confident in the pocket. He and the Miami offense had been kept off the field for most of the second quarter by two time-consuming Army drives. The more impressive of the two, a punishing six-minute drive, ended in familiar fashion—with Trent fumbling away the ball at the Miami 24-yard line. So instead of a two-touchdown lead and an Army team committed to Coach Ellerson's rallying cry of winning the next snap, Erz saw in the eyes of a young secondary the realization that if they kept making mental mistakes, Dysert was going to make them pay. He sought out cornerback Lamar Johnson-Harris and safety Hayden Pierce, both freshmen, and encouraged them to focus on their assignments, to stay in their coverage.

When Trent got the offense rolling at the start of the second half, however, the free-floating anxiety in the locker room at halftime looked like it was for nothing. Raymond Maples burst over the right end for twenty-two yards, and then Trent kept the ball and scooted up the left sideline forty yards to the Miami 18-yard line. He went right for ten more, and two plays later he busted two tackles and fell into the end zone. When Alex Carlton kicked the extra point, Army was up 28–14.

Miami then took to the air and mounted a thirteen-play, fifty-two-yard drive that was slowed briefly by Erz charging through the Redhawks' line to sack Dysert. But Miami kept moving the ball and arrived at Army's 4-yard line and looked ready to come away with some points. On second down, after Miami running back Erik Finklea fought his way to the goal line, Army safety Tyler Dickson put his helmet on him and knocked the ball loose. Andrew Rodriguez scooped it up and stumbled out to the 9-yard line.

He was swarmed instantly by Erz, Nate Combs, and a mob of gold helmets. The celebration bounced to the Army sideline, where more players crashed into A-Rod. Suddenly, there was silence. The referees had decided to review the video of the play to see if Finklea was already down when he lost the ball. In some of the replay angles, it looked as if his knee was already on the ground when the ball was knocked loose.

It took three tense minutes, but the referees could not find conclusive evidence that Finklea was down, so the ruling on the field stood. Army kept the ball. It had been a long time since the breaks had gone the Black Knights' way, but this one had, and they had momentum and a two-touchdown lead. But they couldn't move the ball and had to punt.

By now, Dysert had figured out how to attack the Black Knights' secondary. As time was winding down in the third quarter, the Miami quarterback needed barely two minutes and four passes—the last one for a seventeen-yard touchdown—to march the Redhawks sixty-one yards and narrow Army's lead to 28–21. But on offense, the Black Knights could not get out of their own way. On first down from their own 29-yard line, Trent handed the ball to Raymond Maples, who ran through a big hole for six yards. He was fighting for extra yards when the Redhawks' C. J. Marck pulled the ball loose and jumped on it at the Army 35-yard line. It was the tenth fumble the Black Knights had lost this season.

Dysert needed only one minute and twenty-nine seconds to find Miami receiver Andy Cruse all by himself in the back of the end zone for a nine-yard touchdown on the first play of the fourth quarter. The score was now tied at 28–28, and the Miami fans inside Yager Stadium rose to their feet, knowing they had Army back on its heels. With the offense still sputtering, Army punter Chris Boldt boomed a forty-yarder that was downed by a gaggle of Black Knights at the Miami 2-yard line, raising cheers on the Army sidelines.

Miami did not stay in a hole for long. Dysert connected on back-to-back passes to Willie Culpepper, and the Redhawks were out to midfield. Johnson-Harris, Pierce, and the rest of the Army secondary were utterly confused, and on the next play Dysert dropped back briefly, then tucked the ball in his arm and took off down the left side of the field before running out of bounds at the Black Knights' 24-yard line. Coach Ellerson called a time-out, but the players were wide-eyed as they came to the sideline. Their confidence was shot, and Erz knew it. He urged his teammates to relax and focus, hoping the defense could turn things around.

The Black Knights stuffed Erik Finklea on a run on first down, and then A-Rod broke up a pass intended for Miami's Kendrick Burton. Erz and his teammates were closing in. On third down and six from the 20-yard line, the Black Knights needed to stop Miami. Dysert dropped back and, for a moment, nobody was open. He shuffled in the pocket once, twice, then fired a pass into the end zone and into the outstretched hands of Miami receiver Nick Harwell. It was Dysert's twenty-fourth completion of the game for 342 yards, and his third touchdown in the second half.

The score was now 35–28, and Miami was on the verge of winning its first game of the season. With 7:05 left to play, Trent and the offense had plenty of time to force the game into overtime, and they went to work quickly. Trent hit Malcolm Brown with a twenty-three-yard pass to the Miami 45-yard line. Malcolm, Trent, Raymond, and then Jon Crucitti each ran the ball, and suddenly the Black Knights were on Miami's 31-yard line. On third down and nine, Trent went to the air again and this time found Austin Barr for nine yards and an inch, giving Army a first down on the Redhawks' 24-yard line.

Malcolm was tackled for a three-yard loss, but Trent came right back with a pass to Patrick Laird for another fourteen yards and a first down on the Miami 13-yard line. But now the Redhawks defense stiffened. First, Raymond was tackled for a two-yard loss and then a pass to Crucitti gained just a yard. When Trent gained another yard on third down, Army was faced with fourth and twelve from the Miami 15-yard line.

With twenty-five seconds left to play, the Black Knights

had to go for it. They needed seven points to send the game into overtime. Twice earlier in the game, Army had gone for it on fourth down and converted. They needed eleven yards, and everyone in Yager Stadium knew that the ball was going into the air, especially the Miami defense. Trent took the snap, backpedaled, and was sacked immediately by Miami's Jaytee Swanson. The game was over. It had taken five games and a furious comeback for Miami to get its first victory for its new coach. But they got it, and Coach Treadwell was singing the Miami fight song with his team before an appreciative crowd at Yager Stadium.

"We were overdue to sing the fight song," Treadwell said afterward, with a huge smile. "Being an alum, I knew the words. If we win, I'll sing it as many times as they want."

Trent was devastated. The Black Knights' offense had done everything he and Max had thought they could do. They rolled to 326 yards on ground; 99 of them Trent had legged out himself. He was eight for nine passing for 124 yards. But Army had blown a fourteen-point lead in the second half by doing exactly what Trent had sworn to avoid—giving the ball away. Two fumbles. Army was halfway through its season and had a record of 2–4, which could have been, no, should have been 4–2. Just as they did against San Diego State, the Black Knights had found a way to give Miami the game instead of taking a game away.

This one hurt. Erz had felt it coming at halftime and watched the game unravel before his eyes. He wondered just how many more things could go wrong. He knew that somehow he had to help stop it from happening.

"It's terrible to have the ball go down the field," he said. "Give them some credit, but we're better than that. We've got to be."

# 16

<hr />

"Let's make this absolute commitment, regardless of the situation, regardless of the scoreboard, regardless of what happened last week, that we are going to treat every game like a season unto itself."

—Coach Rich Ellerson, October 11, 2011

Steve Erzinger knew what the previous year's Army football captains would have done if the Black Knights were below .500 halfway through the season. So did Max Jenkins and Andrew Rodriguez.

"Steve Anderson would have called guys out and started beating on them," said Erz.

"It would have happened before now," said Max.

"We can't do that with these guys," said A-Rod.

The captains had gathered in Max's office in Bee Barracks to determine the best way to proceed in what was becoming a disappointing season. The senior captains were frustrated. The second-half collapse against Miami had especially bothered Erz because it had played into what he considered one of the myths of Army football.

"I get tired of hearing that we are not a fourth-quarter

team," he said. "That we don't have enough depth and we wear out. Or we don't have enough talent or the kind of offense to catch up when we're behind."

Army's recent history suggested there was some truth to these perceived failings, but one of the key components of Coach Ellerson's plan to overhaul the culture of Army football was making them not true. As hard as it was to say aloud, Max, Steve, and Andrew understood that losing and excuse making had become ingrained in the football program over the past fifteen years. They had signed on with Ellerson to rid Army football of its fatalism, of its acceptance that the Black Knights were always outgunned. They were gaining on that goal, too.

Over the past three years, they had helped a team that had previously been hopeless win five games in 2009 and triumph in a bowl game the following season. Obviously, things were not going the way they had hoped so far this year, but Max, Steve, and Andrew were resolved to find a way to salvage this current season and leave the Army football program in better shape than they found it. Admittedly, the captains felt hand-cuffed. They had inherited a far less experienced group with a more fragile team dynamic than the one they had played on the previous year.

Eleven seniors had started on the 2010 Black Knights and another half dozen had recorded significant playing time. They were talented and tight and the stars of the team. They also supported each other unconditionally. Steve Anderson could call out Erz or anyone else and count on his fellow Firsties to speak with the same voice. They were the most respected members of the team. The current class of seniors was small in number as well as stature. Erz was the second leading tackler in the nation and the anchor of the Black Knights defense. Andrew was the only other four-year player starting, and admittedly he was only a shadow of the player he had been two seasons earlier, when he swarmed the field with abandon. Just being able to play one more season was a significant accomplishment for A-Rod.

The offense belonged to the Cows—Trent and Malcolm Brown—and the young running backs like Raymond Maples and Jared Hassin. Max knew he was a respected voice on the team but also understood the limits of his influence as a backup.

The three captains had come to Max's office to weigh their options and settle on a tone to set for the remainder of the season. All were frustrated enough to yell and scream at some of their teammates, but each was smart enough to know that this would be counterproductive, especially for the Plebes and Yuks, who were learning on the fly. Besides, it was not in any of their natures to play the heavy. Instead, they were going to declare that it was a new season and that each member of the team was accountable from here on in.

"The young guys are grown up. They have all the experience they need after six games," said Andrew.

"No wiggle room, no more excuses," said Steve.

Army was off the coming Saturday and would not play again until October 22 in Nashville, against Vanderbilt University. The Black Knights had yet to win on the road, and the Commodores were an improving team in the mighty Southeastern Conference. Still, the three captains settled on two goals and a plan for attaining them. Max, Steve, and Andrew first were going to meet with Coach Ellerson. Then they would speak with Trent Steelman, offensive guard Matt Villanti, linebacker Nate Combs, and cornerback Josh Jackson—all were Cows; all were respected voices in the locker room. The message was to be succinct. The Black Knights were going to win four of their last six games to become bowl eligible. They were going to defeat Air Force and Navy and win the Commander in Chiefs Trophy for the first time since 1996.

Were both beyond their grasp? Probably. But Max, Steve, and Andrew knew their Army football legacy was at stake, and they intended to aim high and fight like hell to get there.

Coach Ellerson knew that his team needed a fresh start as well as a chance to recover physically. He had laid out a light schedule for the next two weeks. Max, Steve, and Andrew had met with him and told him what they had in mind for the remainder of the season. They told him that they had already held a meeting with some key teammates and were going to hold an all-players meeting to ensure that everyone was on the same page for the season's final push.

Ellerson was as optimistic a coach as there was in the nation, but he knew that five of their next six opponents were better than his team. No one needed to study the film to come to that conclusion. Vanderbilt was perhaps the fastest team Army was going to see all year. Rutgers was undefeated in the Big East Conference. Temple had one of the best running backs in the country in Bernard Pierce and mean, massive linemen on both offense and defense that had helped it land atop the Mid-American Conference. And the Black Knights had not beaten Air Force in five years or Navy in nine. Ellerson knew that his captains were disappointed, but he admired their resolve and believed that they were doing a fine job of keeping the team together.

Halfway through the season and nine months into my time at West Point, I understood how immense the challenges were for Ellerson and his team. Before each game, I had walked the field during warm-ups and marveled at what I saw. Not once did it look like the Black Knights were heading into a fair fight. Northwestern, San Diego State, Miami—even Tulane—had bigger and better-cut linemen as well as sleeker and shiftier running backs. The players on the other teams looked like real-life college football athletes, down to the braids and tangled locks that tumbled out of their helmets.

The Black Knights? They looked like refugees from the golf and water polo teams with a few well-conditioned wrestlers thrown in. When they took their helmets off, the high and tight haircuts made them look like members of a 4-H club. I also knew that on every college football Saturday the Black Knights were one of just three teams in the nation—along with Navy and Air Force—who could say that every one of their players had been up before dawn and had spent the previous week going to challenging classes and studying late into the night.

They did all this in a place steeped in some of America's most important history and with a unique mission—to train young men and women to be Army officers who lead soldiers into armed conflicts with the knowledge that often many of them will not survive.

No wonder Coach Ellerson was unwavering in his belief in his players, his Army team. Ellerson was a passionate orator who reached into a grab bag of metaphors in an effort to touch his team. One of them had especially tickled Andrew Rodriguez and endeared Ellerson to the rest of the seniors as well. It was about what outer space aliens might find if their ship one day landed at West Point and observed the players on his team. Ellerson had goosed it with variations and riffs over the captains' careers. But he always conjured the same image of the hardest-working, hardest-loving, and toughest band of brothers there ever was playing a game they loved. In Ellerson's vision of Army football, his players were equal parts fearless gladiators, erudite gentlemen, Zen masters, and calloused, lunch-bucket-toting steelworkers.

Mixed up or not, it was an apt metaphor about what goes on each day at the United States Military Academy. Virtually every cadet is dropped off here as an alien to a culture that they have forty-seven months to make their own. The fact that some cadets add football or other varsity sports to an already brutal schedule is simply remarkable. That the Academy's motto of Duty, Honor, Country is embroidered into all aspects of campus life is a singular achievement. It is embodied twenty-four hours a day, seven days a week by the Army officers who are TACs and are instructing them in the classroom and by the generals who are frequent visitors here.

Instead of the NFL stars at the practices and along the sidelines of their former schools—Michael Irvin at Miami or Reggie Bush at USC—at Army practices and games, there are Medal of Honor recipients like Sergeant Petry and four-star generals like Martin E. Dempsey, the current chairman of the Joint Chiefs of Staff. Earlier in the week, General Ray Odierno, the chief of staff of the Army, had come to practice. At six feet five inches and with a head as shaved and domed as the nation's Capitol, Odierno was an awe-inspiring presence in the middle of more than one hundred cadets. He was a member of the class of 1976 who had been recruited to play football but injured his knee and finished his athletic career as a pitcher for the West Point baseball team.

Instead of making millions as an athlete and enjoying a post-athletic career as a broadcaster, Odierno had gone on to earn a master of science in nuclear effects engineering and a master of arts in national security and strategy. Over a thirty-

five-year career, the general had held some of the most important military assignments and had his hand in some of the
most admired feats in modern military history. He had served
as the commanding general of United States Forces–Iraq and
was one of the primary architects of "the surge" into Baghdad
and putting into practice the counterinsurgency strategy that
dramatically decreased violence in Iraq in 2007 and 2008 and
is credited with turning the war around. General Odierno spoke
to the team mostly about the toughness they had already displayed and how it would serve them well throughout their military lives and beyond.

Larry Dixon had been bowled over by the general's warmth,
commanding presence, and wise words. Odierno hadn't taken
the hurt out of his Plebe experience, but the general had given
Larry a glimpse of why he—and all cadets—had chosen and
endured at West Point.

"He gave me a vision of what I could become," Larry said,
"of what I can accomplish, of what I want to be."

It was moments like those when Coach Ellerson knew that
he was doing the job that he wanted in a place where he was
needed. During his tenure as superintendent, Douglas Mac-
Arthur had given the football program stature as well as a man-
date to be another classroom where character and leadership
was taught and nurtured. Ellerson was the son of a West Pointer,
a brother to two others, and Army was his ground zero for his
love of football.

"Consistently good, occasionally great," was how Ellerson
articulated his on-field goals for Army football.

Losing was no fun—it never is for a professional coach. But
Ellerson was building something here, and he was as proud of
the wisdom and maturity shown by his seniors as he was of the

talent and growth he was watching blossom from his younger players. He agreed with Max, Steve, and Andrew.

"You are no longer a rookie team," he told his players at practice. "You've been around the block together. We may be a little bit physically immature, but we are a veteran outfit. We're not going to use that word, *immature*, about ourselves anymore. We have been there, done that."

So he asked to forget about the first six games. It was last season.

"Let's make this absolute commitment, regardless of the situation, regardless of the scoreboard, regardless of what happened last week, that we are going to treat every game like a season unto itself."

# PART FOUR

# FIRSTIE YEAR

# 17

"We're all busy whether it's with school or leadership positions or football. It's about managing your time and getting after it. You learn that quick here or you don't last."

—Max Jenkins, October 29, 2011

Major Anthony Bianchi was definitely more fired up for the
football game coming up on Saturday than the presentation he
was about to hear from Steve Erzinger and two of his classmates in Bianchi's Applied Systems Design class. Sometimes a
team needs a victory plain and simple, and that was why the
Fordham Rams were on Army's schedule. Fordham had just
started awarding athletic scholarships in football but played
in a class below the big time, the Football Champion Subdivision (FCS), or what used to be called Division I-AA. Since 1978,
Army had scheduled at least one FCS team, usually from the
Patriot League, where it was a member in every other sport. It
offered their smaller opponents a decent payday, and it gave
the Black Knights a breather from a crushing schedule.

It was the one autumn Saturday that Army—at least on
paper—got to face an overmatched opponent. And the Black

Knights had taken care of business, going 50–10–1 against the designated cupcakes over the last thirty-three years.

Major Bianchi had been an offensive lineman on the 1996 Army team, which had gone 10–2 and set the program record for most wins in a season. Those Black Knights had gone into the Independence Bowl against Auburn ranked No. 24 in the nation. This year was the fifteenth anniversary of that season, and Bianchi, as chairman of the reunion committee, had been wise enough to choose the Fordham game for their gathering. Bob Sutton had been the Army head coach, and he was coming up from New York City, where he was now a coach with the New York Jets. Bianchi was expecting forty-five or so members of the team to show up for the game.

"I'm pumped," Bianchi told a small class in Mahan Hall on Wednesday, October 26. "I've got six guys staying with me. They start coming in tonight. I've got to stop by the liquor store and make sure I have enough beer."

Army's 1996 team was the high-water mark for the football program over the two disappointing decades before Coach Ellerson's arrival. Bianchi's team had a talented option quarterback in Ronnie McAda and had made the most of a soft schedule—Ohio, Yale, and Lafayette—and had also handled Air Force and Navy authoritatively.

Though they got waxed, 42–17, by a Syracuse team led by the future NFL quarterback Donovan McNabb, the Black Knights very nearly shocked the Tigers of Auburn in the Independence Bowl. Army had been down 32–7 when it put up twenty-two unanswered points in a frantic fourth-quarter comeback. Army rushed for 257 yards in the game, but it was McAda's uncharacteristic 148 yards passing that keyed the Army resurgence. His 30-yard touchdown pass to Rod Richardson with 1:27 remaining closed the gap to 32–27, and when

Bobby Williams bulled over to complete a two-point conversion, Auburn's lead was down to three points.

When Army defensive back Matt Rogers recovered an onside kick at the Tigers' 45-yard line, the stage was set for a monumental upset. The Black Knights drove the ball down to the 10-yard line, and, with time running out, McAda spiked the ball to stop the clock and allow Army to attempt a field goal that would tie the game. Senior kicker J. Parker had made seventeen straight field goals from inside the 30-yard line and was eighteen of twenty-one overall in the regular season. He had not missed inside the 40-yard line all season. But Parker caught his right foot in the ground and the attempt sailed wide right. Auburn had cheated overtime and won, 32–29.

Just the memory of that season and bowl game—heartbreaking or not—still gave Bianchi a massive smile and intermittent chills. He was looking forward to reliving the moments throughout the weekend with his teammates.

Now, however, it was time for Steve and his fellow Firsties Anna Stein and Vaughan Michael to tell Major Bianchi how they were going to reduce the Academy's carbon footprint and make West Point more efficient by harnessing the energy created at Arvin Gym, where all the cadets work out. This assignment was an exercise in planning and presentation.

"Or briefing, a skill constantly employed and always appreciated at all points in the chain of command," said Major Bianchi with a wry smile that got knowing laughs.

Anna was en route to medical school, and Vaughan was also an accomplished student; he was weighing various graduate schools in a variety of disciplines. Steve handled his portion of the briefing with command and concise detail. It was when he stood alongside Anna and Vaughan, however, that his sole regret about his time at the academy surfaced—his Plebe year, when he had misguidedly chosen the path of "C's for degrees." Branch Night was six weeks away, and Steve was trying to get his mind around the fact that he was unlikely to be selected for the Infantry and that he had no one to blame but himself.

He wasn't exactly depressed, but he was definitely down a little bit. The trip to Nashville to play Vanderbilt the previous week had not gone well. The new season-unto-itself that Steve, his fellow captains, and Coach Ellerson had promised began a lot like the first half of the season that they were trying to forget. The prospect of Steve and Max and A-Rod gathering at West Point fifteen years from now for a reunion of a bowl team looked increasingly unlikely. The Commodores beat them soundly, 44–21, and amassed a season-high 530 yards against the Black Knights.

Jordan Rodgers was making his first start for Vanderbilt, and Army's young secondary made him look like his older brother—the Green Bay Packers' Super Bowl–winning quarterback Aaron Rodgers. He rushed for ninety-six yards and a touchdown and threw for another.

Trent Steelman, meanwhile, was tackled in the closing minutes of the first half and had to be helped off the field by two Army trainers when he could not put weight on his left leg. Neither Max nor freshman quarterback Angel Santiago could gear up the Black Knights' offense. Trent's streak of thirty-two straight starts, a record for an Army quarterback, not only was going to end against Fordham, there was concern that, man of steel or not, he was perhaps lost for the season.

Steve, too, was out for the Fordham game. He had pulled his right hamstring against Vanderbilt and aggravated the labrum, the cartilage in his left shoulder, which had limited his range of motion all season and made excruciating pain his constant companion. There was a hitch in his step and a grimace on his face as he walked stiffly out of Major Bianchi's classroom to Thayer Hall and his History of Military Arts class.

There is a certain Harry Potter aura to the school days at the United States Military Academy—partly due to the post's gray, Gothic architecture that seems to haunt rather than inhabit the bluffs above the Hudson River. The fact that virtually everyone is in uniform, too, gives it an otherworldly feel. There definitely is a sense that a chosen few are being taught, if not exactly a dark art, a dangerous one.

The classrooms are cozy and intimate, rarely with more than seventeen students and usually even smaller. Often, cadets stand behind their tables or desks as instructors click through Power-Point presentations or question them on material. Standing is an accepted, even encouraged, way to ward off falling asleep, which is a real possibility, especially among Plebes and Yuks. An ill-timed snooze is the most benign way for a cadet to find himself marching on Friday and Saturday afternoons among the Shammers in full dress, rifle in hand, for hours at a time.

The faculty are on the young side, most of them rotating into the classroom from Iraq and Afghanistan with harrowing stories and telltale scars. Conversations among instructors and cadets can drift from economics to improvised explosive devices to the world's great religions to counterinsurgency. The fact that the cadets are here to be warriors, and warriors often die, is always front and center.

Major Chris Dempsey was one of those young professors who had served tours in Iraq. A member of the class of 2000, Dempsey also had a master's degree in military history from North Carolina State University. But he and his colleagues eventually circle back to Iraq and Afghanistan. In Dempsey's case, he had perhaps even a deeper understanding of the Army's modern conflicts—his father is General Martin Dempsey, the chairman of the Joint Chiefs of Staff.

Major Dempsey taught Military Arts, and one lesson was on "breadth, depth, and context" at the Battle of Shiloh. Besides the fact that Ulysses S. Grant is among West Point's most famous—if not greatest—graduates, Dempsey used his early battles in the Civil War to teach a lesson about the importance of will and certitude. Grant had earned celebrity as "Unconditional Surrender" Grant when he forced the Confederate general Simon Bolivar Buckner—his close friend during their days at West Point—to do just that at Fort Donelson in Tennessee, handing over an entire army of more than 12,000 soldiers. Six weeks later at Shiloh, in the bloodiest battle ever fought on the North American continent to that point, Grant was victorious in another unlikely battle.

"Grant moved hard and fast and believed destroying the opposing army at whatever cost was essential to victory," Dempsey told his students.

His pronouncement struck a contemporary chord with Steve and his classmates. The previous week, President Barack Obama had announced that all remaining troops in Iraq were going to be withdrawn by the end of the year, declaring that the nearly nine-year war that had drawn on the military service of more than one million American men and women was over.

"The last American soldiers will cross the border out of Iraq with their heads held high," the president had said. "That is how American military efforts in Iraq will end."

President Obama made the promise from the White House, and its breadth, depth, and context had been sliced, diced, and picked over in the days since by everyone from political pundits to grateful parents to hawks and doves. There were a myriad of reasons and arguments put forward: it was political grandstanding; it was surrender; it was a clear-cut victory. The 2012 election race was on. The Arab Spring was in full bloom. The war in Afghanistan was next, or American troops would never be out of there. Osama bin Laden was dead, as was Al Qaeda. No, Al Qaeda was alive and well and regrouping.

Among the cadets, the president's declaration that the war that had defined their journey to West Point, and their time there, was soon to be over was mainly met with disappointment.

Even Steve, sore and dejected about the football team and anxious about his future, could not hide his disappointment.

"You come here to serve and deploy," he said. "It's war for real, and it would be awesome to be a soldier, an officer, under that kind of pressure."

Max Jenkins and Andrew Rodriguez were about as cool-headed as one could be at twenty-two years old, but neither of them could hide his regret, either. At first, Max feigned disinterest and philosophical acceptance.

"You can't spend time thinking about things you have no control over," he said. "That's always been out of my hands."

But quickly he pivoted to the unrest in Egypt, Syria, and across the Middle East. He had read that the Army was sending more and more troops to its base in Kuwait, and his spirits started to rise. "There's going to be plenty of demand for us," he concluded.

Andrew's sister, Amy, was in Iraq right now. He worried about her but had not spoken to her about life there or her experiences in Haiti, where she had served previously, or anything Army at all.

"We try not to talk about business," he said.

He was the son of a four-star general who had fought there
as well, a fact that Andrew did his best to play down throughout his time at West Point. Inevitably, however, an instructor
or new TAC or a visitor to campus would find him to tell a
story about a situation or meeting with his father in Iraq or
Afghanistan. He confessed it often was strange hearing these
intimate stories from strangers, especially knowing that they
had taken place during one of his father's long absences when
Andrew was at home, or at West Point, missing him and worrying about him. Now, he was seeing an opportunity to be like
him slip away.

"It's tough to see," he said of the president's announcement.

Steve, Max, and Andrew had just spent the past forty
months having every ounce of their fiber torn down and over-
hauled. They had endured the classroom pressure and absorbed
the ways of military life until it became second nature. They
had spent countless hours in the woods on impossible missions
where they made inevitable mistakes that would have gotten a
squad, a platoon—even a whole battalion—killed.

They were leaders, men of character, who had duty, honor,
and country coursing through their veins. They had been
painstakingly rebuilt into the military equivalent of Ferraris or
Porsches. Now, the world's biggest Grand Prix track was gone
and closed.

Max Jenkins could not believe what he was seeing—snow, the
wet and swirling kind, and it was stacking up in snow banks
in the stands and across the field at Michie Stadium. He beat
back a wave of panic. They wouldn't call off the game against
Fordham because of weather, would they? It had been gor-

geous most of the week, sunny and crisp with the leaves offering a kaleidoscope of autumn colors in the Hudson Valley.

On Saturday, October 29, however, West Point and most of southern New York awoke to a winter storm even though it was fall. It was senior day and Max was making his first start at quarterback for Army. His mom, Felicia, and his sister, Regan, were in town. The Erzingers, the Rodriguezes, and the families of all the seniors were here for the final game they would play at home at Michie Stadium. The Firsties were checking off another milestone on their journey to become second lieutenants.

It was even more bittersweet for Max. He thought about how much his father would have enjoyed this moment—these last two years, really. How proud he would be of Max beyond the football achievements. He was brigade deputy commander. He had been to Germany. He was in the top 5 percent of his class. For a game at least, he was Army's starting quarterback.

"I know he's here with me," Max said.

Army and Fordham were going to play, though not in front of the biggest crowd in seventy years at Michie Stadium, as had been projected before the snowstorm. The game was sold out, and the Academy had braced for an overflow of New York–based tailgaters. Fordham was less than an hour from West Point, and its alumni were largely in and around the New York metropolitan area. By offering scholarships for football, the Jesuits who ran Fordham had made a commitment to football that had excited its alumni.

Besides, this was a rare and novel meeting between the two schools. They had played only twice before. The first time was on October 24, 1891, and Army's 10–6 win over Fordham was the first victory in Army history. The second meeting was on November 5, 1949, when Army defeated the Rams, 35–0.

No, only the hardiest souls were on hand when Max led the Black Knights onto the field. And those were the cadets, four thousand strong of them, bundled up in their camouflage combat gear with hoods cinched tight over their heads. Because of the inclement weather, all leaves had been canceled and the cadets were postbound. The pregame warm-ups had been a blast. The field was buried in white, and the snowplows zigzagging on the field could not keep up with the snowfall. The Black Knights were slipping and sliding during warm-ups, tossing snowballs at one another and getting wet and cold.

Major Bianchi and his 1996 teammates were keeping warm at Kimsey and in the warm suites and boxes of Army's most deep-pocketed supporters. Coach Ellerson had coached in the Canadian Football League, but he had never been on the field when the flakes were flying as heavy as it was at kickoff. He liked his team's energy and attitude before the game. They were having fun, something sorely lacking recently. He wanted his team to have a confidence-building victory.

It was a 3:30 p.m. kickoff, but the stadium lights were on and flickering when the Black Knights crunched onto the field, pumping their legs higher and higher as they ran the gauntlet of Plebes who welcomed them on the field. Even that abused and fatigued bunch was having a ball. Sheets of snowflakes were swirling throughout the sky. It was as if the Black Knights had run into a surreal and shaken snow globe. There was laughter bubbling through their mouth guards and grins beneath the face masks. It was like they were all ten years old again.

"It's like Christmas," said Max, who was struggling to put a game face on. "How can you not be excited?"

By game time the grounds crew had given up. They grabbed shovels and were trying to keep the yard lines clear enough so the referees had some sense of where the action was on the field. It was obvious on the first play that it was going to be a long afternoon for Fordham. Raymond Maples took Max's handoff and motored thirty yards straight downfield to the Fordham 38-yard line. Behind, several Rams spun their wheels in the snow in pursuit. Five plays later, Max kept the ball and scored from one yard out.

Fordham relied on the passing game, and the conditions made it impossible for Rams quarterback Ryan Higgins to keep his feet in the pocket, let alone throw through a blizzard to an open receiver. On the Fordham sideline, Coach Tom Masella knew he was in for a long day. It had started that way at dawn when he awoke to the snowstorm. Masella understood the magic of West Point. Since the preseason, he had told his team about the history of Army football, and he had promised his players a once-in-a-lifetime experience. Win or lose, Coach Masella wanted them to feel what it was like to perform before a packed house in the midst of the ghosts of Grant and Eisenhower and Blanchard and Davis. He was bringing every player on his roster and intended to play them all so that someday they could tell their kids they had played against Army. But on the way north, one of the Fordham team buses broke down and forty of his players had been stranded.

Now, Coach Masella watched as Army scored on its first five drives and took a 42–0 lead into halftime. Max had run for two touchdowns and threw for another, a perfect 30-yard strike to Anthony Stephens, who looked like a Clydesdale churning through the snow. Raymond Maples had rushed for 159 yards and Larry Dixon rolled to 85 yards and a touchdown. Even the Black Knights' defense scored when linebacker Nate Combs picked up a fumble and slid into the end zone.

When it was all over, Army had accumulated 544 yards of offense in a 55–0 victory that was capped off by an epic snowball fight in the cadet section of the stands. They had stayed for the whole game, braving the elements and singing the fight song as the empty bleachers in every other corner of the stadium were getting piled high with the white stuff. In fact, one of the loudest cheers of the afternoon rose when a sold-out crowd of 39,481 was announced over the public address system. That many had bought tickets but few had come.

Fordham's Coach Masella kept to his word, though, and made sure that all his players got onto the field. They did so as the Rams were being shut out for the first time in six years, allowing fifty points for the first time in more than a decade.

"I was really disappointed in the fact that it was not what it could have been for our kids," Masella said afterward. "It's not the experience I wanted them to take away from coming up to West Point, but it's no one's fault but Mother Nature's, so you can blame Mother Nature for this."

In the Army locker room, the smell of snow and wet clothes hung in the air as looks of satisfaction clung to the Black Knights' flushed faces. Max had been the man of the hour in the postgame press conference, with Coach Ellerson praising him for being a "wily, confident, old veteran" who had always made the most of his limited opportunities. Max deftly handled the reporters' questions, including one about how he juggled his duties as deputy brigade commander with football and school.

"We're all busy whether it's with school or leadership positions or football," he said. "It's about managing your time and getting after it. You learn that quick here or you don't last."

He moved quickly to share the credit for the victory with

his running backs, his offensive line, and the defense, naming as many names as he could call forth.

"It was my first snow game and a lot of other guys' first, too, so you might as well go out and embrace it," he said. "It was definitely a ball."

Below, in the Army locker room, no one was in a real hurry to leave. The players were tired, and the snow had eliminated all options but returning to their rooms. They dressed slowly. When Max returned after the news conference, he stood before his locker as a slow procession of his teammates came by to offer their congratulations. Even the Plebes who did not know Max that well stopped by and were happy for him. Max had made an impact among all constituencies, which was the gift that Major Hequembourg had recognized in him and had helped Max to develop even more as a key leader in the Corps of Cadets.

Major Hequembourg believed that Max was ready to do great things in the Army and had laid the foundation to become a career military officer. Hequembourg was going to be proud to have been associated with Max.

Steve and Andrew and the rest of Max's Firstie classmates were the last ones through to offer bear hugs and big smiles. They had gone through a lot together, and while they were not having the final season they had imagined, these Saturdays at Michie Stadium were always going to be cherished. It had been a memorable afternoon.

# 18

"It's a fight. It's an absolute fight that we're having, not only with our opponent but with ourselves. We need to learn to play well without a net, without any margin for error. The fact is there is no net. We don't have any reserve firepower that's going to make up for some of those miscues."

—Coach Rich Ellerson, November 7, 2011

They were lined up for blocks on River Avenue beneath the elevated subway tracks in front of Yankee Stadium—columns of cadets clad in gray, many of them bleary-eyed from the combination of having to be here at 8:00 a.m. and the late hours they had kept the night before in New York City. There was no better destination for a cadet at the United States Military Academy than a weekend in Manhattan, and the game against Rutgers that afternoon had given them a reason to enjoy the city that never sleeps.

It was Saturday, November 12, just short of a full year since the day that my son, Jack, had urged me to go find the good guys. Now, he and his mother, Mary, were with me on the street watching the young men and women, all stiff collared and gleaming brass, marching into Yankee Stadium. We were hardly alone. Folks, many of them in Rutgers gear, were tumbling out of Billy's and Stan's and the other taverns on River Avenue, lining up five and six deep. Most applauded and some even waved flags. There's something about a uniform and a commitment to service that touches even the most hard-hearted of us.

The past year had absolutely exceeded our family's expectations. We had wandered every inch of West Point, had drunk in its history and traditions, and had even hosted a Saturday afternoon tailgate, which is a special joy for a midwesterner transplanted to Manhattan. Little things had made a big impression. Mary came to enjoy being called "ma'am" and I looked forward to my e-mail correspondence with cadets who unfailingly signed off, "Very Respectfully."

Jack and I found the good guys in the biggest way, and the simplest thing I can say about the United States Military Academy is that if my son were accepted there someday, I'd be the proudest father in the world—as well as a terrified one.

Unfortunately, for anyone who follows sports, big-time college football had remained on its scandal-ridden track. In the previous week, the iconic Penn State football coach Joe Paterno had been fired, and the university's president, Graham Spanier, was forced to resign after a longtime assistant coach, Jerry Sandusky, was charged with sexually abusing ten boys over a fifteen-year span, including in Penn State's football complex. There had been a prior investigation and allegations over the years, including a lewd encounter witnessed by another assistant coach, that the university trustees believed Paterno and Spanier had not done enough to address. The national debate about the outsized importance of college football in our universities and our culture was growing noisier and more bitter.

Coach Ellerson, however, had no time to think about such

questions. He remained in his in-season vacuum and was absolutely tortured by his team's most recent collapse the previous Saturday against Air Force. For the Black Knights, it was going to be another year without a Commander in Chief's Trophy; the Falcons had captured their second straight win, having dispatched Navy earlier in the year.

In short, Army gave away a 14–0 halftime lead and lost to Air Force for the sixth consecutive time in all too familiar fashion, 24–14. The key play came at the end of the first half, when Army's Scott Williams twisted his way toward the goal line for what would have given the Black Knights a 21–0 halftime lead. Air Force defensive back Josh Hall punched the ball out of Williams's arms and out of the back of the end zone for a touchback. This was the third time in the half that the Black Knights had driven inside the Falcons' 20-yard line and gotten no points. Twice before, Army had failed to convert on fourth down.

In the third quarter, Coach Ellerson watched his team self-destruct in a hurry. Air Force started the second half with a thirty-seven-yard field goal, then forced Army to punt. On their next possession, the Falcons scored a touchdown and completed a two-point conversion to draw to within 14–11.

On the next drive, Max Jenkins fumbled the snap, which soon led to a tying field goal. Then, on fourth down from Army's own 36-yard line, Coach Ellerson gambled and called a fake punt. But Army wide receiver Justin Allen fumbled the pitch from the up back, and Air Force recovered the ball at the Army 14-yard line. Four plays later, Falcons quarterback Tim Jefferson scored from a yard out, and Air Force was up 21–14 with fifteen seconds left in the third quarter. But there was more agony to come. Early in the fourth quarter, Air Force's Jon Davis stripped the ball from Jared Hassin and returned the fumble to the Army 19-yard line, which led to a field goal and a 24–14 final score.

On the following Monday, Coach Ellerson remained devastated. In fact, Major Bagley and other members of the football office had never seen him so low. The coach held the longest staff meeting in his tenure, but there were more mysteries than answers.

"What's breaking our heart," Ellerson began, "what's got us staring at the wall all night are missed opportunities, turnovers, and penalties, and those do carry over. That is the poised, present, disciplined football that we need to make a reality. We need to be able to do it with the game on the line."

Finally, Coach Ellerson decided to get into his team. It was time for him to be honest and direct, but he had to be careful not to lose them. He had been part of teams that had crumbled under frustrations and recriminations.

"Once the 'screw yous' start going back and forth in the room, you've lost them," he said. "There is great effort out there. There's a hard try without a try well."

As soon as the team meeting opened, Coach Ellerson telegraphed to his team that he was hot. He did not like the amiable chatter and laughter going on. He wasn't going to talk over them, and he told them so. The room fell still.

Coach Ellerson said that it was time for Army football to talk with one voice. His voice. They had to believe in him and what he was trying to do with his program. They had to exorcise the negative outcomes from their consciousness. He picked up steam as he spoke. His face reddened. He told them that he knew they were tired of hearing him say that they had to be in the moment for each play. For the next snap. But they had no other choice because the best weapon they had was their minds. Talentwise, they were merely human.

"It's a fight," he said. "It's an absolute fight that we're having, not only with our opponent but with ourselves. We need to learn to play well without a net, without any margin for error. The fact is there is no net. We don't have any reserve firepower that's going to make up for some of those miscues.

"When we have an opportunity we need to close the deal. When we have a chance to make a play we have to make it. We have to get this right."

Had Coach Ellerson gotten his team right? He had no idea, but the week before the Rutgers game they had practiced as well as they had all season.

Long before warm-ups, the players from Rutgers were walking from foul pole to foul pole of Yankee Stadium and taking photos of themselves and each other on what for even the most casual baseball fan is hallowed ground. It is true that this Yankee Stadium was just two and a half years old and that twenty-six of the New York Yankees' twenty-seven championships had been earned at the old ballpark across the street. This corner of the Bronx was famous, however, and Rutgers coach Greg Schiano brought his team here earlier than he had ever brought one to a game. He urged them to take photographs, enjoy their surroundings, and then return to their locker room and forget about it all. Army, even at 3–6, was too dangerous.

The two schools had a long and cherished rivalry in football going back to 1891, Army's second season of football. Rutgers led the series, 19–18, and had won the last seven meetings against the Black Knights, including a 23–20 overtime win in 2010. Coach Schiano had done what Ellerson was trying to do—resurrect a program that had become a punch

line. He was now in his eleventh season and had compiled a
65–66 record. He had taken the Scarlet Knights to bowl games
in five of the six previous seasons, and the 2011 team was 6–3
and contending for a Big East title.

This was technically an Army home game, but half the
crowd was sporting the red and gray colors of New Jersey's
flagship state university. Yankee Stadium has long held a prom-
inent role in college football, and Army is the primary reason
why. Army's games were national events and in one instance
even became a national security asset. During the Battle of the
Bulge in World War II, American troops were surrounded and
being infiltrated by English-speaking German spies dressed as
American soldiers. In an effort to tell friend from foe, unfamiliar soldiers were asked to give the score of Army's 1944 game
with Notre Dame. Everyone (every American, at least) knew
that top-ranked Army had walloped Notre Dame, 59–0, at Yankee Stadium.

In 1928, it was at Yankee Stadium that Knute Rockne
supposedly urged his Notre Dame team to "win one for the
Gipper" in its game against Army, with a passionate speech
about a deathbed conversation with the former Notre Dame
great George Gipp, who had died of pneumonia eight years
earlier. The Army–Notre Dame games in Yankee Stadium from
the 1920s to 1940s had also created the Fighting Irish's "subway alumni," the first-generation Irish, Italians, and Poles who
rode the trains from the five boroughs to cheer players with
names like their own—and who in subsequent generations
sent their sons and daughters to Notre Dame.

In 1946, Yankee Stadium was host to what sportswriters
at the time dubbed the "Game of the Century" between
No. 1–ranked and undefeated Army and No. 2–ranked and
undefeated Notre Dame. The game ended in a 0–0 tie, primarily

because Red Blaik and Notre Dame coach Frank Leahy had their teams play too cautiously. In fact, Blaik later told the former Notre Dame running back Terry Brennan that he had "choked" in the face of all the hype, which was too bad in a game that featured four Heisman Trophy winners. Doc Blanchard had won his the previous season and his teammate Glenn Davis was about to be named the 1946 winner. Notre Dame's Johnny Lujack won the trophy in 1947 and his teammate Leon Hart won it in 1949.

On this Saturday morning in November, however, the Rutgers players were more in awe of the fact that they were playing on the home field of Derek Jeter, Mariano Rivera, and Alex Rodriguez than that they were playing against a team that was better than its record.

The emotional tone of the afternoon was set at the coin toss, when Eric LeGrand led the Rutgers captains to the middle of the field in his motorized wheelchair. He wore a red stocking cap and a jersey with his No. 52. Eric had been an irrepressible symbol of hope in the year since his collision with Malcolm Brown. His stated goal was no less than to inspire the world. Doctors had believed at first that the spinal cord damage, two fractured vertebrae, and paralysis would make Eric a quadriplegic on a respirator for the rest of his life. Within five weeks after the accident, however, Eric had resumed breathing on his own. Over the summer, he turned to his Twitter account, tweeting out a picture of himself on his feet, braced by a metal frame. He was doing some commentary on the Rutgers television broadcasts, and two weeks earlier, amid the surprise October snowstorm, Eric had led the Scarlet Knights onto the field at Rutgers's stadium for the game with West Virginia. An ax rested in his lap, a nod to Coach Schiano's motto, "Keep chopping."

"So I left tire tracks in the snow yesterday as I led my team out next time will be footprints," read his tweet the following day.

Malcolm went out to midfield with Steve Erzinger, Max Jenkins, and Andrew Rodriguez, and Eric responded to his pat on the shoulder with a broad smile. They had remained in touch, and Malcolm's visit with Eric in the hospital over the summer had deepened their bond. Still, it was a heart-piercing moment for both young men. And as the Army captains returned to the sideline, Steve and Andrew threw comforting arms over Malcolm, making sure he was all right.

For this game, Coach Ellerson had decided to make a change at quarterback: Angel Santiago, a Plebe, was getting the start over Max Jenkins. It was a football decision plain and simple. Angel was more talented and explosive. Max knew the offense and ran it proficiently, but the Black Knights needed more of a threat at quarterback—someone like Angel who could keep the ball on the option and turn it upfield for seven or ten yards, as Trent Steelman was able to do. At five feet eleven inches and 195 pounds, Angel was a quicker version of Trent. He was Army's future quarterback, and the future was now. In fact, football aficionados would see, during the next sixty minutes of football, much of what the future of Army football was going to look like. Angel was the ninth Plebe to start for Army this season, and he would be taking the snap from another Plebe, Ryan Powis, and handing it off to a third Plebe, Larry Dixon, who also was getting the start against Rutgers.

Max was disappointed, but he put those feelings aside. He slipped on his headset and prepared to keep his head in the game and be ready to play at a moment's notice, as he had his whole career at Army. Trent, meanwhile, was trying to figure

out how he could be most useful to his teammates. He had
suffered a high ankle sprain and some stretched ligaments.
After thirty-two games as a starter, being unable to play had
left him at a loss, but Trent was continuing his quest to be a better teammate. He was in a supporting role now, and as uncomfortable as that was, he wanted to contribute to his team. For
Max, Trent knew that meant offering quiet consultation. For
Angel, Trent suspected that he needed to be more encouraging.

"I'm trying to figure out what makes him tick," he said. "I
want to help, not confuse him."

Angel, indeed, looked tentative the first time he carried the
ball, on the second play of the game. He barely had taken the
snap from Ryan when he backed up and was swarmed immediately by Scarlet Knights for a two-yard loss. The next play,
however, Larry Dixon sent a message to Rutgers and the more
than thirty thousand people crowded into Yankee Stadium
that the Black Knights had come to compete this afternoon.
He took Angel's handoff and burst through the middle of the
line, then into the secondary, and was in full flight for fifty-five
yards with a squadron of Scarlet Knights in pursuit. His strides
were getting shorter and sod was flying in his wake—a product
of turf having to be laid over what usually was a dirt infield—
until he finally stumbled and fell on the Rutgers 3-yard line.

Larry had a smile beaming like a lighthouse as he was
swarmed on the sidelines. The smile remained on his face as he
watched the replay in high definition on the giant screen that
flickered over the Bronx in what usually is the outfield. This was
the big time, and the Black Knights were going to enjoy it.

On the field, Angel kept the ball and got to the 1-yard line,
but on second down he was swarmed again for a five-yard loss.
One more time, Angel kept the ball on the option and managed
to make up the ground he had previously lost. So now it was

fourth and one from the 1-yard line, and Coach Ellerson decided to kick a field goal. Army had tried and failed to pick up critical short yardage at Air Force, and the coach was taking no chances against Rutgers. When Alex Carlton drilled an eighteen-yard field goal through the uprights, Army was on top 3–0.

The next time Army got the ball, Angel ran the triple option as if he had been doing it all his life. He kept the ball and scooted upfield for eighteen yards. He jammed it in the stomach of Jared Hassin, who ran for ten more yards. Over the next eleven plays, Army pushed around the bigger Rutgers line for fifty-eight yards, arriving at the Scarlet Knights' 2-yard line. Again, Army couldn't get the ball across the goal line, and Alex returned to the field to kick a nineteen-yard field goal to put the Black Knights up 6–0.

The points were welcome, but touchdowns would have been better, especially because it was unlikely that the Black Knights were going to contain the Rutgers offense for long. They were an experienced unit that had averaged twenty-seven points and 322 yards a game. In junior Mohamed Sanu, the Scarlet Knights featured one of the best wide receivers in the nation.

Rutgers's opportunity came late in the first half, after Army gambled on fourth and two from the Rutgers 40-yard line, and Angel was tackled for no gain. Rutgers quarterback Chas Dodd then drove the Scarlet Knights sixty yards in eight plays. Running back Jeremy Deering got loose for nineteen yards on first down, and then Dodd found Sanu alone in the secondary for sixteen yards and down to the Army 25-yard line. Deering plowed through the Army line four more times, putting Rutgers on the Black Knights' 3-yard line. When Dodd dumped a three-yard pass to fullback Michael Burton, it appeared the

Scarlet Knights would take a 7–6 lead into halftime. But Rutgers kicker San San Te yanked the extra point wide left. It was all tied at 6–6.

It was the best half of football Army had played since the Northwestern game, and in the plush locker room of the New York Yankees the Black Knights knew it. They gathered in the middle of the room as if they were unworthy of the Yankees' polished wood locker stalls and the soft chairs that guarded them. Angel could not slow his internal motor down and was vibrating in a folding chair. Nate Combs hollered at his teammates on defense not to fold. The coaches were scribbling furiously on whiteboards as the players fidgeted and paced. There was an air of anticipation. The Black Knights were not only playing well but they had rediscovered the joy in the game.

So had Coach Ellerson. He blew into the middle of the room and was short and sweet. "Next snap, one voice," he said. "Leave that clock and scoreboard to me. It belongs to me."

He paused, glaring into the eyes of his players.

"You lucky guys get to play the next snap," he said. "Are you tough enough to do that?"

Rutgers apparently had made some adjustments at halftime and found a renewed commitment to the pass. On the opening drive of the second half, quarterback Chas Dodd picked apart the Black Knights' secondary, finding Sana three times for twenty-five yards to the Army 38-yard line. He then threw a perfect strike to a streaking Brandon Coleman who used all of his six feet six inches to stretch and snatch the ball out of the air over an Army defender and score. This time Te converted the extra point and Rutgers was on top 13–6.

The Black Knights offense had stalled for much of the third quarter, but Erz and A-Rod had the defense amped up. It was putting pressure on Dodd on pass plays and shutting down

Deering and the other Rutgers running backs. With 1:20 left in the third quarter, Army's Thomas Holloway stepped in front of a pass intended for Sanu, intercepted it, and ran it back nineteen yards to the Rutgers 36-yard line. Holloway was immediately mobbed by his teammates, and as they tumbled toward the Army sideline it set off a chain reaction of fallen bodies.

Angel, Jared, and Larry made Rutgers pay for their mistake by pounding down the middle of the field for thirty-six yards. It took Army nine plays and four minutes, but Larry blasted over the middle for a two-yard touchdown, and the Black Knights were back in the game, except that Alex Carlton missed the extra point, so Army trailed 13–12. There are many ways to lose football games, and in the previous nine contests the Black Knights had found most of them. They had given the ball away; they had been outplayed; they had missed kicks.

But with a little more than seven minutes left in the game, the Black Knights experienced one of the crudest setbacks of all. Army's Kyler Martin had just intercepted Dodd, stopping a Rutgers drive and giving the Black Knights the ball near midfield. It had sent the spirits in the cadet sections soaring. In fact, all afternoon that corner of Yankee Stadium had been rocking, partly because their team was playing well in a very tense game. It also had to do with the stadium's booming sound system blasting pop and hip-hop music and the high-definition big screen. The cadets were having a ball seeing themselves bust dance moves that—minus the dress grays— were as hip and polished as what anyone would see later that night in the New York dance clubs. They were enjoying themselves, and the rest of the crowd was enjoying the show they put on via the big screen.

Now it was second and long, and Angel was running parallel

to the line when he saw the end commit to him and threw a perfect pitchout to Stephen Fraser on the edge. The sweep was on and the blocking was beautiful. As Scarlet Knights tumbled all around him, Stephen streaked between them fifty-one yards right toward the cadet section before being caught at the Rutgers 1-yard line. It was bedlam as the cadets roared and jumped up and down in the stands, and the Black Knights celebrated on the sidelines.

Suddenly, however, a hush fell over the stadium. There was a yellow flag down on the other side of the field. The referees huddled. When they broke, the call was tripping by Frank Allen; away from the play, he had gotten tangled with Rutgers defensive back David Rowe. It was amazing that a referee had even seen the offense, which certainly had nothing to do with Stephen's run. Instead of first and goal on the 1-yard line, the run was called back. Army failed to get a first down. So Chris Boldt trotted onto the field to punt for the Black Knights.

He handled the snap, dropped the ball to his foot, but just as he made contact Wayne Warren of the Scarlet Knights dove and blocked the punt with his chest. The ball squirted on the ground, and Rutgers's Jordan Thomas scooped it up and ran it back thirty-two yards for a touchdown. In less than thirty seconds and on the fall of a yellow flag, Army had gone from potential victors to certain losers.

By the time Jawan Jamison scored in the closing seconds on a fifty-six-yard run to seal Rutgers's 27–12 victory, everyone on the Army sidelines knew Coach Ellerson was right. There was no margin of error for the Black Knights. Captain Clarence Holmes, Army's defensive line coach, walked down the sideline and put his arm on Lieutenant Colonel Gaylord Greene's shoulder. Both had played for the Black Knights—

Holmes graduated in 2003 and Greene in 1993. They had seen this too many times before.

"It's real easy when you got the cats," said Holmes, nodding at the Rutgers players celebrating at midfield.

"We gave it our all," replied Greene.

Both men continued to stare across the field not consoled in the least. "We always do," said Holmes finally.

## 19

"This is our night to become members of the proud and distinct communities that comprise the awesome warfighting machine that is our Army."

—First Captain Charles Phelps, December 1, 2011

As it had so many other years, Army's season came down to a single game, the most important one on its schedule for the past 112 years—the annual tilt with the United States Naval Academy. It was the Game of Honor. It was a civil war. It was America's Game. It was the greatest rivalry in sports. It answered to all of those titles, but in reality it was two brothers beating the hell out of each other for sixty minutes and then embracing at the end and daring anyone else to take on the other.

It had been a disappointing season—there was no other way around it. As Steve Erzinger, Max Jenkins, and Andrew Rodriguez gathered in Max's office to assess where the heads of their teammates were and to figure out how to mount one more push, the stark reality could not be denied. The Black Knights had won only three games. They were not returning

to a bowl game. The only way to salvage the season, and perhaps even their Army football careers, was to do something
the Black Knights had not done for nine years: beat Navy! The
three captains knew it was their last chance. As grueling as their
life at West Point had been, they all agreed the time had gone
awfully quickly.

"I was talking a lot to the younger guys," said A-Rod, "and
it always seems like you're going to have more chances, but
the time goes by so fast."

*Beat Navy!* Those two words were stenciled on the roofs of
barracks and buildings on campus for passing airplanes to see.
They were painted on black and gold signs stuck in the yards
of the officers who lived on post. It was a phrase that Plebes
learned on Reception Day, immediately after "sir" and "ma'am,"
and they would utter it tens of thousands of times over the next
forty-seven months. It was how West Pointers greeted each other
here and abroad.

It was part of Coach Ellerson's DNA as well. He grew up in
a West Point family and among Academy graduates at bases all
over the world. He was in Germany when his brother John
played for Army in the 1960s, and he listened to the Army-
Navy game on the radio. As a kid, he looked forward to the
rivalry with the ardor of a teenage boy waiting to give a girlfriend a first kiss.

"Sing second," was his team's rallying cry. Ellerson wanted
it so bad for them, especially the Firsties.

Over the summer, the coach had held a reception for the
incoming two dozen or so international cadets who come to
West Point each year. One was from Tunisia, another was
from Jordan, and each was out of his country for the first time
and had been at West Point for only a few days.

"Beat Navy!" were their first words upon meeting Ellerson.

"They didn't know football from third base," the coach said. "By the time they come through the gate and get to my house, though, they know I better beat Navy. They don't know what that means, but they know I better do it."

While Army enjoyed the upper hand against Navy during the 1990s, hard-fought victories were the rule, with the Black Knights' seven victories in that decade coming by a total of just twenty-four points. But since 1996, the results for Army had been grim. Navy had captured twelve of the past fourteen meetings and had taken the series lead, 55–49–7. The Midshipmen's current nine-game winning streak was the longest in the series for either academy.

This season there would be even more time for the anticipation to build, because the game had been moved back a week in order not to compete with the higher-profile championship games in the Southeast, Big 12, and Atlantic Coast conferences. The service academies' broadcast partner, CBS, wanted the game to dominate its own Saturday, and so it was scheduled for December 10. CBS increased its rights fee to get the academies to agree to the change, but Army and Navy now risked the possibility of missing out on an invitation to a bowl game. Invitations were sent out the first week in December, and if either team had been sitting with five victories, it is doubtful that a bowl committee would wait to see if it beat its oldest rival to reach the six wins needed to be bowl eligible.

Bowls, especially the lesser ones, needed time to sell tickets and mount advertising campaigns. They could not afford to wait to see if Army beat Navy, or vice versa, to become bowl eligible. This question turned out to be a moot point in 2011 as neither Army nor Navy had had a successful season. With a 4–7 record, Navy was not going to a bowl game for the first time in eight years.

Having three weeks to practice before the Navy game did allow the Black Knights to recover from whatever bad habits they had indulged in over Thanksgiving as well as get some badly needed time to heal their broken bodies.

Steve Erzinger spent more time on the phone with Danielle, and they talked about everything but football. Not only was Danielle an athlete who understood Steve's frustration and the effort it took to discuss it, but their romance was blossoming, and, frankly, they had better things to talk about. Steve's parents had flown Danielle out for the Air Force game as a surprise. She was coming to the Navy game, and Steve intended to spend part of his Christmas leave in Nashville. Neither wanted to get ahead of themselves, so for now they had agreed simply to enjoy their final year in college—and to enjoy each other's company.

Andrew, meanwhile, tried to watch a couple of movies on his computer. The stoic scholar had a liking for guy comedies like Adam Sandler's *Happy Gilmore* and old-school classics like *Caddyshack*. Max was reading up on the Marshall Islands, the Micronesian nation in the middle of the Pacific just west of the International Date Line and just north of the equator. He was heading there after Christmas to complete interviews and a site survey for an engineering project for which he and a team were supposed to develop a master plan for the capacity development of Ebeye, the most populous island in the Marshalls, taking into account its economy, government, infrastructure, health, and education.

Being on post had also put the captains back in touch with the routines that mark the passing of time at West Point. It had been months since Steve had passed through the cadets' central area and seen fifty, sixty, or even seventy cadets marching back and forth in full dress in the courtyards between the barracks on weekend afternoons. He had been either at a hotel or on a football field during the season's weekends.

The marching cadets wore the passive expression of toy soldiers, and as their boots clicked on the stone, they sounded like a giant metronome. They were not doing it for fun. They were marching off hours of punishment that they had received for offenses ranging from falling asleep in class (five hours) to underage drinking (eighty hours). It was a wearying, mind-numbing exercise that Steve wasn't going to miss.

"I've had fifteen hours total," he said. "I've known guys who have had more than one hundred hours."

It was a day trip down to Washington, D.C., and back. Coach Ellerson, Steve, Max, and Andrew were participating in a news conference with Navy coach Ken Niumatalolo and the Midshipmen captains on the Wednesday after Thanksgiving. The game was being moved from its traditional home, Philadelphia, and being played at FedEx Field in Landover, Maryland, just outside of the nation's capital, for the first time. The stadium was a lot closer to Annapolis and the United States Naval Academy, but the close proximity of the Pentagon and several Army bases ensured that the crowd would be evenly divided between fans of the two academies.

As soon as they arrived at LaGuardia Airport in New York, Andrew split from his teammates, found a table, and pulled out his books and a calculator. Max was getting something to eat and Steve was looking at magazines in the gift shop. The coach was curious, so he looked over Andrew's shoulder.

"You need some help?" he asked his player, half joking but also looking for an opportunity to show he knew some stuff.

Andrew shrugged. Ellerson leaned in closer. The best he

could tell was that it was some sort of calculus. He couldn't have helped Andrew if he had tried.

"Can I get you a Coke or something?" Ellerson offered weakly.

Andrew kept his head in the books. It was these moments that the coach was reminded of how much he loved his job. This was what college athletes—all young people—should act like, should aspire to. Ellerson admired Steve, Max, and Andrew. He also owed them. They had taken his blueprint for Army football and brought it to life. Each day, they had stacked up wins in the classroom, in the chain of command, and back in the barracks. It had been a tough year for them on the field, but his captains had kept the team together and Army football would be better for it for years to come.

"It's the way home," Ellerson said. "I can't prove it yet, but I'm telling you this is working. The scoreboard can't validate that for me just yet, but as impatient as we all are and as painful as those Saturdays were, this is happening. It's happening because guys like them, in the face of adversity, when it got hard to hold on to that culture, fiercely they did just that."

At the Army Navy Country Club in Arlington, Virginia, Ellerson and Niumatalolo greeted each other warmly. They knew other well. In 1983, Ellerson was the coach who had recruited Niumatalolo out of Honolulu to play quarterback at the University of Hawaii. Niumatalolo was in his ninth year at Navy, and this was his fourth year as its head coach. He was a decade younger than Ellerson and a whole lot more voluble.

Ellerson and Niumatalolo liked each other and would continue to remain friends despite the fact they now had to see each other once a year in a meeting where one of them inevitably would have to leave disappointed. The Navy coach, too, felt deeply for his players and what was at stake for them.

"When you recruit people here, and you're in people's homes, that's always in the back of your mind," Niumatalolo said. "Yeah, the education is second to none, there's great career opportunities and being able to provide for your families, but there's also a chance they might have to pay the ultimate sacrifice. They'll be in harm's way—that's a reality."

Unlike Ellerson, Niumatalolo had had no idea of the magnitude of the nation's most storied rivalry when he was growing up. He was a Mormon and thought nothing could top the passion of the matchup between the University of Hawaii and Brigham Young University. In 1995, however, he was an assistant in Annapolis and was absolutely blown away by his first Army-Navy game. He remembered the team bus pulling into Veterans Stadium in Philadelphia and looking out the window to Army's Corps of Cadets in their gray uniforms and Navy's Brigade of Midshipmen in their black uniforms, waiting for the traditional march in.

"It sent chills down my spine," he recalled. "It's kind of like a civil war or something. You could've cut the intensity with a knife, it was so thick."

The Navy coach was surrounded by high achievers as well. John Dowd, an offensive lineman, was Navy's first two-time academic All-American, boasting a 3.91 grade point average in mechanical engineering. Dowd was a finalist, along with A-Rod, for the William V. Campbell Trophy, given for outstanding achievement in football and academics. He had started twenty-four consecutive games at right guard and wanted to become a submariner despite the fact that he was six foot four and 260 pounds.

Alexander Teich, the Navy captain, was one of twenty-eight midshipmen selected to enter Navy Seal training. "I kind of always want to be leading from the front," he said. "They're the tip of the spear, the first ones into the fight, and that's kind of my mentality. I want to be the first one into that fight leading my men."

Now, however, the Navy captain's mission was the game that had been circled on his calendar each year—the one that he lay awake each night in bed waiting to come. Teich was 3–0 against Steve, Max and Andrew, a fact that none of them discussed as they made small talk at the Army Navy Country Club. He also had a 3–1 lead in bowl games. There was no bowl game for Navy this year, but Teich made it clear to the cadets, to everyone, that this did not matter.

"This game is way bigger than a bowl game," Teich said. "There's so much passion in this game. A bowl game is kind of a celebration. This game is how football's meant to be played."

The following night was Thursday, December 1, and the Firsties filed into the auditorium at Ike Hall to the strains of Lee Greenwood's "God Bless the USA." They wore their camouflage combat uniforms, tight smiles, and, for some, a worried look. It was Branch Night. In the next few minutes, they would find out in what branch they would begin their military careers. Their performance over the past forty months determined where they would serve over the next five years. The combat arms branches (Air Defense Artillery, Armor, Aviation, Engineers, Field Artillery, and Infantry) were the most desirable, and they had to be 80 percent men and 20 percent women. The support branches—Adjutant General, Quartermaster, and Finance Corps—could be up to 20 percent men and up to 80 percent women. Only 2 percent of these Firsties—about twenty—were allowed to choose medical school, and no more than 1 percent, or ten, could select a different branch of service, such as the Navy or the Air Force.

The TACs and the other officers wore hats and carried T-shirts with their branch insignias, to be given to their new members. They were all in a good mood and needled one another about why Armor was better than Infantry and vice versa. They handed, or flung like Frisbees, the envelopes that contained the Firsties' destinies. It was a festive night, one that First Captain Charles Phelps urged his classmates to relish.

"This is our night to become members of the proud and distinct communities that comprise the awesome warfighting machine that is our Army," said Phelps in his opening remarks.

It also was a sober night. For many of the cadets, it was where the dream they had as boys and girls and the choice they made as teenagers to come to the United States Military Academy came into real focus. For some of them, it may have been for the first time. If any of them had any doubt what they had signed on for, Phelps reminded them with a quote selected from Robert A. Heinlein's novel *Starship Troopers*.

"You are now going through the hardest part of your service," read Phelps. "Not the hardest physically but the hardest spiritually, the deep, soul-turning readjustments and re-evaluations necessary to accept the call of duty. The noblest fate that a man can endure is to place his own mortal body between his loved home and the war's desolation. This is an immutable truth throughout all time, for all men and all nations."

Brigadier General Theodore D. Martin, the Academy's commandant, went for a lighter mood and flashed a slide of a genie's lantern on the big screen behind him.

"I know some of you have been locked in a decisive battle with the dean's forces for the past forty months," he said to laughter. "And it's been touch and go."

Indeed, there were going to be some disappointed Firsties when the signal was given for them to open their envelopes. Branch assignments were determined by class rank, and the cadets in the middle or low range had been sweating over the lot of their future life for months. Among them was Steve Erzinger. He gripped the envelope in his right hand and tried to focus on General Martin. It was hard.

Steve had decided against extending his Active Duty Service Obligation an additional three years. His first choice was Infantry, but with only 239 slots available, he knew he was hoping against hope. He had next chosen Armor, which had absorbed the calvary in 1950. Steve liked the idea of becoming a cavalry officer doing reconnaissance missions. In swagger, Armor was second only to Infantry, and there were Armor officers in Ike Hall now wearing black Stetsons, the unofficial head gear of tankers and the like.

General Martin was an entertaining master of ceremonies, tossing off one-liners as a slide of each branch appeared and the number of Firsties it was accepting.

"Fifty lucky cadets will go to Air Defense Artillery, where the saying is, 'If it flies, it dies,' " he said.

"Well, we're not going anywhere without orders," he said, as a slide of officers sitting at desks popped up. "Twenty-three lucky cadets will join the Adjutant General's Corps."

General Martin, however, saved his best stuff for last when a tank appeared on the big screen and showed that ninety-nine Firsties would be accepted into Armor.

"Every team must have a captain, a master, someone to call the shots," said Martin to raucous cheers from Armor officers. "And for that we have an elite group of warriors, I might add, devilishly handsome and winning young officers."

He paused and let the laughter roll over them.

"We call them tankers," he said. "Tanks. They're awesome. And ninety-nine super lucky cadets will join Armor."

Then, General Martin reached beneath the podium, pulled out a Stetson, and placed it atop his head. He was an Armor officer.

Finally, the order was given to open the envelopes. Steve took his time. Cheers and a smattering of groans echoed throughout Ike as Firsties either greeted or cursed their fates.

"Armor," Steve murmured and then looked up with a smile. He was relieved and headed out to the lobby where the Armor officers were waiting to greet their new ranks. Each branch had a gathering place, and there was food and beer waiting below at Ike's Café.

At the base of the auditorium stage, 239 Firsties were being congratulated by officers as well as congratulating one another for being selected to Infantry. Max was there and so were Andrew and the rest of West Point's most accomplished cadets. They were alone in the auditorium and suddenly playing on the screen was a scene from the movie *300*, the ultraviolent retelling of how a small force of three hundred Spartans heroically fought to the death against hundreds of thousands of Persians.

It was the scene where King Leonidas hailed his men as the bravest and best in the world and that death would be their likely reward. When it ended, an infantry officer stood up on stage. He didn't look much older than the soon-to-be second lieutenants. He wanted them to understand who they were, what they were about to become, and what they probably will have to face.

"We are the best of the best," he said. "We are the tip of the spear. We are warriors."

# 20

"This is the one. Have fun out there."

—Coach Rich Ellerson, December 10, 2011

Steve Erzinger had been confined to his hotel room—its bathroom mostly—for the past forty-eight hours. He had the flu, or something. He could not keep food or liquid down and was unable to sleep. He read all night and into Saturday morning, closing his eyes every now and then, praying that the prescription medication would finally kick in. Now his final game against Navy was two hours away and he was on his back on a training table in the bowels of FedEx Field. He was white as bone and could barely keep his eyes open as an IV coursed fluids into his arm. One way or another, he was going to get onto that field.

Outside the training room, the Black Knights' locker room was rocking. Music was blaring and players were swaying and grooving like they were on the dance floor of *American Bandstand*. No doubt about it, they were loose, confident. Even Trent Steelman had replaced his pregame scowl and hunched shoulders with a wide smile and chin-up stride. Beneath his uniform, his ankles, knee, and chest were wrapped and taped like a sausage. He was nowhere near 100 percent, but he was the starting quarterback once again.

"How you feel?" asked his right tackle, Mike McDermott.

"They're going to have to drag me off," said Trent, with a little extra honeysuckle in his Kentucky drawl.

Steve finished a second bag of fluids and then received a cortisone shot in his shoulder. Warm-ups were about to start and he hurried to get dressed. Army was wearing their white jerseys, and Steve looked at the message sewn inside its collar.

"Sing Second," it read.

The stadium was already three-quarters full with the more than eighty thousand people who had set aside a cold, sunny Saturday afternoon to watch the nation's most storied rivalry. The cadets in their dress grays and the midshipmen in their dress blues had marched onto the field an hour earlier and were now seated opposite each other in the end zone. The sidelines looked like a cafeteria at the Pentagon, there were so many generals and admirals walking along them. The White House had announced that Vice President Joe Biden was coming, but the worst-kept secret of the week was that President Barack Obama was going to be in attendance as well.

Nine previous presidents had taken in the game, beginning in 1901 with Theodore Roosevelt. Harry Truman liked it so much that he went to four of them—1945, 1946, 1948, and 1950—and was something of a good luck charm for Army, who won three of those games. Dwight Eisenhower was the only future president ever to play in the game—he started at halfback and linebacker in Army's 6–0 loss to Navy in 1912. But he came just once in his two terms in office. John F. Kennedy, a decorated Navy veteran, was perhaps the game's biggest fan.

"It's easy to pick the real winner of the Army-Navy game: the people of the United States," he once said.

Kennedy was the first president to perform the pregame coin toss, which has since become a presidential tradition. He was set to attend his third consecutive game in 1963 but was assassinated eight days earlier in Dallas. The game was canceled until Jacqueline Kennedy said publicly that it would be good for the nation as well as a tribute to her husband if the game that he loved to watch was played. It was rescheduled for December 7, and Navy won 21–15.

When the Black Knights returned to the locker room fifteen minutes before game time, Steve had gotten some of his color back during the warm-ups, but he looked like he had not gotten any sleep. The players were still upbeat and raucous, as were the Army officers who crowded inside with them. Steve, Max, and Andrew made their way around the locker room to the other Firsties, offering bear hugs and whispered words. This was it for them, their last game for Army, the last time any of them would pad up and play a silly game that they loved deeply.

Andrew kept his helmet on. It had already been an eventful week for him. At a dinner the previous Tuesday at the Waldorf Astoria in New York, he had been awarded the William V. Campbell Trophy, the academic Heisman that had previously been won by the likes of Peyton Manning and Tim Tebow. His mother and father had met him in New York, and they were here today as well for his final game. All those lonely hours of rehab the previous spring and the extra hours in the classroom had paid off. Andrew was going to follow his father in the Army. He had gotten one more season and one more opportunity to beat Navy.

Major Bagley summoned the three captains. It was time for

the coin toss, and President Obama was, indeed, the one who would be doing the flipping. Major Bagley ushered them to the door.

Coach Ellerson floated through the room. He was as relaxed as his team. He knew that he was never going to get a telegram like the one Red Blaik got from MacArthur in 1944 after Army beat Navy, 23–7. "We have stopped the war to celebrate your magnificent success," it read. But Ellerson knew that this Army team could beat that Navy team in the other locker room.

"How much time, Bags?" he asked.

Major Bagley checked his watch.

"Forty-five seconds," he said.

"Major Bags is calling the shots," a Black Knight yelled good-naturedly, turning a loud locker room even louder.

When Coach Ellerson raised his hand and stepped to the middle of the room, the players got quiet. He was smiling as he looked at his team. He knew that they did not need to hear much. He knew what they could do.

"This is the one," he said. "Have fun out there."


Lore has it that the Army-Navy game originated in 1890 when a Navy midshipman challenged an Army cadet to a game. The rivalry almost ended before it had a chance to become storied when the Army-Navy game was suspended from 1894 to 1898; following Navy's 1893 victory, a fracas broke out between a rear admiral and a brigadier general that nearly led to a duel. Neither the Army nor Navy faithful is any less passionate today, but perhaps more than ever in this era of global conflict there is a greater emphasis on the fact that cadets and midshipmen are brothers in arms.

Navy's chaplain, Lieutenant Commander Seth Phillips, a rabbi, reminded those inside the stadium of this brotherhood in his invocation to our "Creator and Coach."

"Here we gather, fans of Army, fans of Navy, fans of this historic rivalry," he said. "Though we are partisan, we are as one in our gratitude to witness this game that brings honor to the concept of student-athlete. We are as one in admiration for these players who at the very apex of their sporting career will put aside the games of youth to serve their country.

"To You who animate all life, we ask for blessing on those who play and those who have prepared them, on those who watch today and on those who must work. And for my brothers and sisters in arms, let this game offer a peaceful respite from war and a reminder of home. Now let us live truly helpful, truly hopeful."

Once the ball was in the air for the opening kickoff, however, the cadets and midshipmen—as well as the two academies' fans—forgot they were on the same side. The Navy faithful got to celebrate first as the Midshipmen, on their first possession, slashed through the Black Knights at will. It was mainly Navy's senior quarterback Kriss Proctor inflicting the damage. He got loose on runs of nine, seven, and six yards to move Navy to the Army 15-yard line near the end zone, where the midshipmen and cadets were sitting.

Proctor was similar to Trent in build but was far more emotional than the Army quarterback. In overtime against Air Force, he ran for a one-yard touchdown, then was penalized for unsportsmanlike conduct after appearing to taunt an Air Force defender. The extra-point attempt, now from the 35-yard line, was blocked and cost Navy the game.

It was first down and the middies were on their feet, certain that Proctor or fullback Alexander Teich was going to punch the ball in for a score to draw first blood. It was Proctor who kept the ball, and as he turned upfield, Army's Jacob Drozd rocked him with a square-on hit, sending the ball to the ground, where Nate Combs was on it in an instant.

Nate came bouncing off the field and was rushed by what seemed to be the whole Army sideline.

"This is our day," Nate bellowed, red-faced. "Our day."

Soon, however, their day looked like too many other Saturdays this season. Just three plays later, Raymond Maples was looking for someplace to run in a backfield suddenly swimming with Midshipmen and fumbled. Navy's Jabaree Tuani came up with the ball on the Army 26-yard line, right in front of a roaring middies section.

Max Jenkins was the first player to reach Raymond, banging him on the helmet.

"Next snap," he said. "Next snap."

On the field, Navy wasted no time. Teich hammered into the middle of the line for four yards, then four more, and then another five yards to reach the Army 4-yard line. On the next play, Steve, Andrew, and Nate rammed up the middle, expecting the ball to come to Teich, but Proctor kept it and jitterbugged into the end zone.

Navy, indeed, had drawn first blood. They drew second as well after Jared Hassin fumbled at midfield in the opening minutes of the second quarter. First, Proctor got outside and scampered thirty-two yards, deep into Army territory. When Navy got to the Army 10-yard line, the Black Knights' defense stiffened and forced the Midshipmen into third down and a long eight yards. Steve, Andrew, and Nate crowded the line. They needed to stop Navy now and force a field goal. Instead, Teich took the ball from Proctor, bounced off one tackle, and bolted into the end zone. In the stands, the Navy section erupted, the midshipmen bouncing up and down, their white hats in hand.

When Jon Teague booted through the extra point to give Navy a 14–0 lead with seven minutes left in the half, a chant—a taunt, really—went up in the middies' section.

"Why so quiet?" they sang out, getting louder with each verse. "Why so quiet? Why so quiet?"

The cadet section as well as the Army sideline were silent. Coach Ellerson was pacing with his head down. The defense was trotting off the field when suddenly on the scoreboard's big screen came one of Navy's spirit videos. Both academies produce them, and they had run throughout the first half. Most are good-natured and inspiring—soldiers in a dusty base in Afghanistan, saying "Beat Navy," or submariners in the Pacific shouting "Beat Army." The student-produced videos are usually humorous and edgy and feature skits showing how weak and unworthy the rivals is—in one, a midshipman is lying on a therapist's couch only to find out the shrink is an Army drill sergeant.

But one video was almost too on point. It showed heartbroken cadets after Army's tenth straight defeat to the Midshipmen. It was not only harsh but it looked all too true. Across the field, some Navy players laughed, while others winced, thinking the skit had gone too far.

On the Army sideline, the video was met by mumbled expletives and visible anger. Virtually the entire crowd of more than eighty thousand had seen the Black Knights dismissed. Trent slammed his helmet on his head and leaned chest first into a group of linemen.

"We're taking this all the way down the field," he said. "This isn't over."

The offense was focused and crisp from the first play of the drive, a tight sweep with Malcolm Brown skipping over a tackler for four yards. Trent handed the ball again to Malcolm, and he picked his way behind blockers for four more yards. The Black Knights had found a weakness on the edges of the Midshipmen's defense. Once more, the ball went to Malcolm, and he juked and accelerated for ten more yards. Ryan Powis, Mike McDermott, the entire offensive line, were sprinting back to Trent in the huddle, leaving fallen Navy defenders in their wake. They were in a groove, opening lanes wide enough for a battleship to cruise through. Raymond Maples and Larry Dixon alternated snaps and banged inside for thirteen yards.

Trent went back to Malcolm, who wiggled through the Middies for two more yards. It was second and long at Navy's 34-yard line when Trent ignited the triple option in a way it had not been done in his absence. He pivoted from under Ryan, shoved the ball in the fullback's stomach, and then pulled it out and glided alongside the line of scrimmage. Malcolm was trailing. Instead of pitching it back, however, Trent slithered around end and into the secondary. He rumbled thirty-two yards to the end zone.

He turned to the Corps of Cadets and let out a roar as his teammates tumbled on top of him. Once more the Army sideline came to life. Major Bagley was grinning beneath his headset. The Army brass, the generals and colonels, were pounding their hands together, as enthusiastic as the cadets.

When the defense took the field, the Black Knights on the sideline raised their arms, asking for more noise. On first down, Alexander Teich was rocked by Jacob Drodz after a three-yard gain. On second down, he collided into a charging Andrew Rodriguez at the line of scrimmage. On third down, Kriss Proctor tried to slide behind his line on a keeper but was collared by Erz and A-Rod. Navy's punt team trotted out on the field and the Army defense bounced off with their arms in the air.

Trent and the offense got the ball back on their own 37-yard line with 2:45 remaining in the first half. The triple option isn't the best offense to mount a two-minute drill, but the Black Knights were bursting with confidence. Malcolm went nineteen yards and into Navy territory on the first play. Next, Trent did something he rarely did: he dropped back to pass and threw a perfect ten-yard strike to Austin Barr on the Midshipmen's 34-yard line. By the time the Black Knights faced third down and three on the Navy 27-yard line, all the people in the stadium were on their feet.

Raymond took Trent's handoff and popped through the line to the first-down marker and then stumbled on for ten more yards and another first down. Malcolm finished off the drive from there, slashing nine yards down to the Navy 5-yard line and then over the goal line on the next play. When Alex Carlton converted the extra point, the score was tied at 14–14, and the chorus of "On Brave Old Army Team" thundered in the stadium.

Navy had time for one play before halftime, and when Nate Combs sacked Proctor for an eleven-yard loss, the Black Knights ran off the field and into the tunnel with everyone from officers to cadets slapping their helmets and yelling their encouragement. During the intermission, President Obama did what his predecessors had made protocol and crossed the field from the Navy side, where he had watched the first half, to the Army side for the second half.

Inside Army's locker room, the Black Knights were certain the president was now on the winner's side of the field. Trent was transported—loud with soaring spirits. Steve looked much better than he had before kickoff, and he huddled with Andrew and the defense. Coach Ellerson had seen something he did not like in Army's kickoff coverage and went straight to special teams coach Joe Ross. Navy's Marcus Thomas had popped off a thirty-six-yard return after that last touchdown.

"I think they are doing something with their wedge," he told Ross. He then picked up a marker and started diagramming what he hoped was a solution.

"Don't worry, Coach," yelled Trent. "This is our day."

Halftime seemed to be over in an instant, and when the doors to the locker room opened there was General Odierno, an ear-to-ear smile, ready to lead the Black Knights back on the field for the second half.

Coach Ellerson had been right to worry about the kickoff coverage. Alexander Teich, who hadn't returned a kick all year, gathered Eric Osteen's second-half kickoff on the Navy 4-yard line, bolted for a seam on the left side of the field, and ran forty-eight yards to the Army 48-yard line. Teich was soon to be a Navy Seal, and indeed he demonstrated that he liked to lead from the front. While Teich played to a fired-up middie crowd, Coach Ellerson dropped his head and stalked the sidelines, agitated. It took the Navy offense just two minutes to carve up the remaining yardage, and the five-play drive ended with Kriss Proctor running the ball in from the 2-yard line. The Midshipmen had retaken the lead, 21–14.

The Black Knights didn't flinch. Malcolm Brown was having a whale of a game, and he was not nearly finished. He ran for thirteen yards on first down, and Larry Dixon battled his way for thirty-one more. This may have been Larry's first Navy game, but on the sidelines he hardly acted like a Plebe. He had been in the middle of every offensive meeting and had roamed the Army bench area encouraging his teammates.

On third down and seven at the Navy 25-yard line, Trent once more dropped back to pass. Malcolm had slipped behind the Navy secondary and was all alone in the end zone. Trent planted his feet and let it fly. Malcolm snatched it out of the air for a touchdown. Alex Carlton kicked the extra point, and the best Army-Navy game in a decade was knotted once again, at 21–21.

Army and Navy were playing emotionally charged and helmet-rattling football. Steve delivered a bone-crushing tackle on Proctor that sent the ball flying. The Black Knights' Geoffrey Bacon dived to the turf to recover it on the Navy 42-yard line. The Black Knights, however, couldn't overcome a fifteen-yard penalty for an illegal block and had to punt.

The Midshipmen clawed back with a time-killing eighteen-play drive that had everyone in the stadium on the edge of their seats. On fourth and one on the Army 20-yard line, Coach Niumatalolo rolled the dice and decided to go for it. When Proctor crouched behind his center, the noise level rivaled the thunder of the four Navy F-18s in the flyover before the game. Only it lasted longer, as first the Corps of Cadets hit the upper decibels of their registers in an attempt to drown out the snap count of Proctor, which was followed by the celebratory roar of the middies as they urged their quarterback on. Proctor heard them and ran six yards downfield for the first down.

At the end of the third quarter, Navy had landed on the Army 14-yard line. It was the Midshipmen who now felt that they could move mountains; when Gee Gee Greene burst through the line, it looked as if he had a path to the end zone.

Army safety Tyler Dickson closed quickly and wrapped up Greene but not before knocking the ball loose.

There was a gasp of hope in the Corps of Cadets and one of despair among the Brigade of Midshipmen. But Greene recovered his own fumble. When Teich blasted eight yards to the Army 2-yard line, Navy had third down and goal for the touchdown. The Army sideline got busy with players climbing on the bench and waving their arms and urging their fellow cadets to get even louder. The Midshipmen's offensive linemen were in their stances when Proctor crouched behind center and started barking out his signals. Suddenly, there was a break in the line—guard Graham Vickers had jumped offsides. The Corps of Cadets had made a big play. The ball was moved back five yards for the penalty, and one play later Navy kicker Jon Teague was sent in to boot a twenty-three-yard field goal. The Midshipmen had held the ball for nearly ten minutes but had only a 24–21 lead to show for it.

The Black Knights had held, and there was a look of satisfaction on the faces of Steve and Andrew and the rest of an exhausted defense as they slumped onto the bench to catch their breath. Unfortunately, they were not there very long.

Junior slotback Scott Williams was among the surest-handed Black Knights, which was the reason he was the main kickoff return specialist. He caught Teague's kick at his own 5-yard line and followed his blockers upfield for twenty-two yards when Navy's Noah Copeland went flying through the air, knocking the ball loose. There was a scramble, but the Midshipmen's Jordan Drake came up with the ball. Williams was devastated and bounced his helmet on the turf. He put his head in his hands as soon as he reached the sideline.

When Proctor was surrounded by Black Knights four yards behind the line of scrimmage and lost the ball, it looked as if

Scott might be let off the hook. But just as it had for Army's previous ten games, the ball bounced the opponent's way, and Teich came up with the ball. Navy was rattled and sent in Teague to kick a field goal. Teague had had a tough year, converting only eight of his thirteen field goal attempts. This time, he proved deadeyed, booting a forty-four-yard field goal to increase the Midshipmen's lead to 27–21 with a little more than ten minutes left to play.

Trent gathered his offense on the sideline. His glare was back, his jaw set.

"We have time and we have moved the ball on them all afternoon," he said. "Let's get this done."

On first down, when Trent kept the ball and bounced off Navy defenders for ten yards, it was clear that he intended to will this team to victory. He was firmly in command, and the offense believed in his will. It was the reason he had won the job as a Plebe and had broken the Army record for consecutive starts. His ankle, knee, chest—everything on Trent was sore, but he was not coming off the field without a victory over Navy.

He kept the ball again and gained three yards, then handed it to Larry for six and Raymond for another first down. On second down, he dropped back to pass to Davyd Brooks thirteen yards downfield on the Navy 40-yard line. There was a feeling of invincibility growing in the Army huddle, on its sideline, and among the hopped-up Corps of Cadets. Raymond slashed off-tackle for six yards. Larry pinballed between Midshipmen for six more. When Malcolm split the Midshipmen for four yards, the Black Knights were at the Navy 24-yard line.

It was second down, and Trent dropped back to pass, but Navy linebacker Matt Warrick had beaten him to the pocket for a sack and a five-yard loss. On third and eleven, Trent turned upfield and looked for an instant as if he had found a hole, but just as quickly he had two Navy defenders on him. He gained four yards to the 25-yard line, and now the Black Knights were facing fourth down and seven.

There was 4:39 left in the game, and Coach Ellerson wanted to think about the play, so he called a time-out. His team needed a touchdown, pure and simple, because there was not enough time to kick a field goal, get the ball back, and get close enough to kick another field goal to send the game into overtime. Coach Ellerson had to go for it, and the ball had to stay in Trent's hands. He had gained sixty-two yards on the ground and had passed for another seventy-seven. He had erased a fourteen-point deficit in the first half and had carried his team downfield and put them in position to win. The game was in his hands.

There wasn't a soul sitting anywhere in the stadium when Trent bent behind center and barked out his signals. He started down the line but didn't get very far. Matt Warrick had gotten through quickly again and wrangled Trent behind the line of scrimmage. As he fell to the ground, the white hats of the middies started bobbing in the air like foam atop the ocean. The Army side fell silent and remained that way as Navy ground out two first downs and ran out the final four minutes of the game.

The tears welled in Trent's eyes as the final seconds ticked off. Others were crying as well. Steve, Max, and Andrew walked to midfield to congratulate Teich and some of the other Midshipmen they had gotten to know on three previous Saturdays. The loss hurt badly, and there was no pride in almost taking down their rival.

"Almost doesn't work, but it's something I have to live with now," Steve said.

He then joined his teammates on a short but miserable walk to the corner of the end zone where the Corps of Cadets waited. The jubilant Navy players followed behind. The Black Knights lined up and stood at attention.

It was time to sing first yet again.

# EPILOGUE

———•————————————•———

"Go Army; beat Navy!"
—Jack Drape, February 11, 2012

We spent part of the morning at the United States Military Academy's museum and much of the afternoon inside the Foley Center throwing around a black rubber football with ARMY emblazoned on its side. Jack was still building forts for his green army men in his bedroom, but he was also developing a strong throwing arm and a taste for all things West Point. Army was definitely his team, and later that afternoon when we watched the Black Knights defeat Navy in basketball, 69–63 in double overtime, Jack held the ball in his left hand and pumped his right fist and said what you say up here.

"Go Army; beat Navy!" he said, as delighted as if he had hit the winning shot himself.

At halftime, Max Jenkins was introduced, along with the rest of the brigade command. They sat together behind the basket, rooting for the basketball team and being constantly interrupted by cadets. The Corps of Cadets carried on long after football season. The previous week, at Post Night, Max and the rest of the Firsties found out where exactly their military careers would begin. He was heading to the Second Stryker Cavalry Regiment—or Second Dragoons—in Vilseck, Germany. It is the longest continuously serving regiment in the Army and is currently deployed in Afghanistan.

But Max was going to be around next fall as a graduate assistant to the football program, helping out in the weight room and at the Academy's prep school. He had no idea whether he would choose the Army as a career.

"I will be honest and say that if I was a betting man, I will be getting out after five or eight years," he said. "This is by no means set in stone. I just feel that I will want to settle down and be a family man. It is difficult to do in the military. That being said, I am keeping my options open and will decide later down the road. Things can change."

In March, Andrew Rodriguez was named the eighty-second winner of the James Sullivan Award, which is given to the nation's outstanding amateur athlete. He was the sixth college football player to win the award, joining quarterbacks Charlie Ward of Florida State, Peyton Manning of Tennessee, and Tim Tebow of Florida, as well as the third from Army, joining Doc Blanchard and Arnold Tucker ('46).

"This award is a tribute to all the people who have helped me throughout my life, especially my family," Rodriguez said. "I had the opportunity to play for all the servicemen and servicewomen who watched us every week. That's who my teammates and I played for, and this award goes out to them."

He was still doing A work as he counted down the days to graduation and his commission as a second lieutenant with the 173rd Airborne in Vicenza, Italy. It was another brigade that was often deployed to the front lines. The smart money was on him following in the footsteps of his father and having a long and distinguished career in the Army. Andrew discouraged the talk. He had been a general's son long enough to have a feel for diplomacy and managing expectations.

"I'm going to do the best I can and take what comes," he said. "I do look forward to what's coming next."

Steve Erzinger was sporting a sling since having the labrum in his left shoulder repaired. In January, he had padded up one last time after being selected to play in the East-West Shrine Game, which was part fund-raiser and part combine for NFL scouts. It meant he got a trip to St. Petersburg, Florida, and a week to extend his college football career. The chance to play alongside seasoned all-stars had been a true joy.

"When you are out there with guys who know what they are doing, you can just relax and let go and enjoy the game," said Steve. "Our bowl team was like that. We were just so young this past season and had so many guys learning on the job that it was always stressful."

Steve had performed well and had gotten some interest from the Kansas City Chiefs and the Seattle Seahawks. It did make him think about what might have been if he had gone to a traditional college and worked mainly on his game.

Steve had no regrets, though. He had been invited to a conference of the Army's four-star generals at West Point the following day, a Sunday, and he was looking forward to it. He also was hanging around through the fall as a graduate assistant before deploying to the Third Brigade, First Infantry Division, at Fort Knox, Kentucky. Steve was beginning to understand that West Point may be a hard place to endure, but it was easy for him to appreciate what it had given him.

"I told the scouts I play for a team called the Army," he said, "and I'm looking forward to seeing if I can do for them what they have done for me."

Max and Steve were going to have some company introducing the prep schoolers and the Plebes into the ways and rules of West Point. Tyson Quink was coming back to help at the prep school. He and his wife, Tera, had become inspirations at Walter Reed—he with his determined rehab and she with her work in the Warrior Transition Brigade. Now they were coming back to the Academy, where they had first met as Plebes.

On March 9, Army held its annual spring intrasquad game in Doughboy Stadium at Fort Benning, Georgia. The stadium was built in 1924 and honored the infantry soldiers, or "doughboys," who died in World War I. Dwight D. Eisenhower was one of the original assistant coaches for Fort Benning's football team. Coach Ellerson was sticking to his way forward for his football program—keeping his players in touch with their final destination in the Army and mixing in some of his hippie coach philosophies. Ellerson also banged the concepts of rest, recuperation, and nutrition into the heads of his players.

They also worked a great deal on holding on to the ball after a season in which they had the distinction of leading the nation in fumbles as well as rushing offense. It was the difference between returning to a bowl game and defeating Navy.

Steve, Max, Andrew, and the rest of the Firsties voted defensive end Jarrett Mackey as the legacy captain for the 2012 season. Jarrett had been a starter in 2010, but he had suffered a season-ending knee injury in the 2011 opener at Northern Illinois. Naming him captain was the final gift that the outgoing senior class had given the Army coach.

"He's the right guy," Ellerson said of Mackey. "Both his contemporaries and last year's seniors were crystal clear on that."

Coach Ellerson experimented with his early morning practices in the spring with the Black Knights hitting the field at 6:55 a.m. He was encouraged by the results, though ten of his running backs missed some or all of spring ball with various sprains or strains. Ellerson had gotten the go-ahead to keep the morning practices intact for the fall, and he had even managed to persuade the chain of command to open some summer school classes for his Yearlings in order to have their in-season loads lightened slightly.

The man who helped him engineer those feats, Major Bagley, was now Lieutenant Colonel Bagley. His promotion had come through, but with it came some bittersweet fruit: "Lieutenant Colonel Bags" was being reassigned to the Pacific Command in Hawaii. Susan and the kids were thrilled. He was, too, though he was having a hard time getting his mind around being so far removed from the game-day rituals.

"I'm going to miss Friday nights in the hotel," he said, "and listening to the staff through the headphones during the game. Those were the two days that made all the other hustling around worth it."

More than five thousand soldiers and their families came to Doughboy Stadium to watch the Armor team defeat the Infantry team, 20–14. The Black Knights had stayed in the barracks the night before. They also attended a basic training graduation and toured the National Infantry Museum before the game.

Trent Steelman made the trip but didn't play. It had been an eye-opening spring for Trent in many ways. He felt the sting of not being named the legacy captain by the outgoing seniors and had made a commitment to being a more benevolent presence on the team. It was clear that Trent was going to be a work in progress right through the moment that he graduated from West Point. He also had had arthroscopic surgery on his knee and was forced to sit out the last week of spring practice. He knew he had one more shot at beating Navy and going back to a bowl game, and he intended to be healthy for his Firstie season.

"The whole day, including the game, was spectacular," Coach Ellerson said. "The guys know some things now about the path they've chosen for their lives and some things about the organization they've joined and the people they're going to serve with, which will set them up for success going forward."

In the game, Larry Dixon caught a nineteen-yard touchdown pass and ran for thirty-two yards for the Infantry team. He would be the starting fullback heading into the fall, and while Plebe life was not necessarily any easier for him, at least it was coming to an end.

After the game, the Black Knights gave their jerseys away to some of the soldiers in attendance. Larry was allowed to find Ethan Sarles and give him his No. 26 jersey. Ethan was Larry's best friend from home and was completing his basic training at Fort Benning. They hadn't seen each other for close to a year. It was a moment that Larry said he would never forget.

"It was a really powerful experience," he said of the day at Fort Benning, and of being a cadet, too. "These are extraordinary guys out here that you are preparing to lead and lead with."

Go Army!

## ACKNOWLEDGMENTS

In 1933, General Douglas MacArthur told the graduating class of the United States Military Academy, "Today you bring to the Army its annual increment of youth, vigor and fortitude," which were "the things that make West Point the soul of the Army." In 1978, General Alexander M. Haig Jr., then the Supreme Allied Commander, Europe, and commander in chief of the United States European Command, offered what he thought was at the core of this national treasure.

"The fundamental virtue of the Military Academy lies in its ability to produce citizens willing and able to subordinate personal interest for the common good," he said in his Founders Day message. "We who are now in the field are confident that you who are preparing to join us will sustain this proud and worthy tradition."

MacArthur's and Haig's sentiments remain true to this day, and the United States is fortunate to have a place like West Point and the young men and women who thrive there. I'd like to thank the Army and the command at West Point for allowing me the unfettered access to the Academy. Every cadet, officer, and civilian was gracious with their time and candor—it is an environment ruled by transparency.

Coach Rich Ellerson embraced this project totally and

welcomed me, as did his staff. Coach Ellerson was passionate about sharing his vision for a football team that embodies the values of West Point and appeals to the best in all of us. He does what he asks of his players—stacks up Ws. The ever busy Major Chad Bagley always found time to give me insight into the West Point experience as well as talk a little sports. Lieutenant Colonel Gaylord Greene was another West Pointer who always had a smile and encouraging word for me.

I wish I could have written at length about each and every member of the Black Knights. It was my privilege and pleasure spending time with the team. Steve Erzinger, Larry Dixon, Max Jenkins, Trent Steelman, and Andrew Rodriguez were extremely generous with their time and remained patient with my questions well into the spring. They truly are among our best and brightest and will be successful in the military and beyond.

In the Academy's public affairs office, Theresa Brinkerhoff was my guide and all-round information guru. Debra Dalton shared the perspective of a parent of a West Pointer. Cadet Josh Cooksey is a family friend and offered insight into everyday life at West Point. Army's athletic director, Boo Corrigan, was an always genial presence. Bob Beretta, the executive senior associate athletic director, is one of the best in the business and is a tremendous ambassador for Army athletics. Brian Gunning was on top of all things Army football. The crew in the sports information office are all top-notch. Thanks to Ryan Yanoshak, Christian Anderson, Pamela Flenke, Tracy Nelson, Mady Salvani, and Michelle Centolanza. Jen Guzman in the football office always met me with a smile. Rich DeMarco, the voice of the Black Knights, and Rich Johnston, the multimedia whiz, helped out tremendously. Sal Interdonato, the Army beat writer for the *Times Herald-Record*, was generous with his knowledge and insight.

Colonel (Ret.) Eugene Palka is devoted to the young men and women of West Point. He also continues to try to make the world of college athletics a better place. He was invaluable in helping me understand the Academy and the role of athletics in its mission to develop leaders of character. He also was kind enough to look over the manuscript and make sure I was accurate in fact and understanding.

I could not have gone looking for the good guys without the indulgence and support of Joe Sexton, the sports editor of the *New York Times*. He has encouraged me to pursue many lines of reporting that have enriched my personal experiences and, I hope in some cases at least, our readers. I am proud to work alongside a talented bunch of editors and reporters in the sports department. I'm gratified that many of them also are true friends.

Alex Ward, the editorial director of book development at the *New York Times*, has been a wonderful supporter and constant source of wise advice. My editor at the Times Books imprint of Henry Holt and Company, Paul Golob, simply made this book better with his keen insights and deft editing touch. Thank you, Paul. His assistant, Emi Ikkanda, kept me on track. I was lifted by the enthusiasm that Maggie Richards, Holt's deputy publisher and director of sales and marketing, had for this project. I appreciate the hard work that she, Melanie DeNardo, and the whole marketing and sales team at Holt continue to give to this book.

Robbie Anne Hare of Goldfarb & Associates has been my friend and agent for a long time now. She brings good cheer and a sharp pencil to all of my projects. Robbie and Ron Goldfarb have been fierce advocates. Thank you.

I am blessed to have good friends here in New York as well as Kansas City and Texas and other random places. You make me laugh and you make my life richer. I am bountifully blessed by a large, often unruly family of Drapes and Kennedys, which includes in-laws and out-laws, and nieces and nephews.

You are big fun and I love you all.

Mary Kennedy and Jack Drape, I am grateful the most for you and how you have enriched every day of my life. Love you, and, yes, I have renewed the Army season tickets.

# INDEX

## ABOUT THE AUTHOR

JOE DRAPE is the author of the *New York Times* bestseller *Our Boys: A Perfect Season on the Plains with the Smith Center Redmen, The Race for the Triple Crown*, and *Black Maestro*. He is an award-winning reporter for *The New York Times*, having previously worked for the *Dallas Morning News* and the *Atlanta Journal-Constitution*. A graduate of Southern Methodist University, he lives in New York City with his wife and son.